Job stress among employees of banking industry

Acknowledgement

"Expression of feeling through words makes them less significant when it comes to making a statement of gratitude"

I have immense appreciation and gratitude towards all those who gave me their valuable blessings, guidance, motivation and esteemed co-operation to complete my research work.

First and foremost, I thank God, the almighty for keeping my faith alive in him and being there by my side in this path towards knowledge with the rod of light.

With immense pleasure and pride, I wish to offer my heartfelt gratitude to my respected supervisor **Dr. Anurag Sharma**, Associate Professor, Department of Business Administration, University of Rajasthan, Jaipur for his valuable guidance, innovative ideas, constant inspiration, untiring efforts and encouragement to complete my thesis work. Without his guidance and persistent help, this research work would not have been possible.

I would like to express my heartiest and sincere gratitude to **Dr. Ashok Kumar Sharma**, Head, Department of Business Administration, University of Rajasthan, Jaipur for the departmental help rendered by him during the progress of the study.

I would also like to thank all the faculty members of Department of Business Administration, University of Rajasthan for their assistance in my research.

I am very much grateful to my respected parents **Shri Ram Kishan Yadav** and **Smt. Kabool Yadav**, my brother **Mr. Mohit Kumar Yadav** for encouraging me and consistently prodding me to work harder. In spite of the trials and tribulations, they never lost faith that I would eventually bring additional pride to them.

My deepest thanks to my husband **Mr. Vipin Yadav** and son **Kushagra Yadav** for helping and inspiring me in various ways, and for always being there with me during the highs and lows of my research work.

I am thankful to all my friends, colleagues and **Mr. Naresh Sharma (Computer typist of the thesis)** who directly or indirectly helped me to bring this project into this final shape.

Also, I would like to thank all the participants in the survey, who willingly shared their values and precious time. I would also like to extend my sincere thanks to University and all my Department committee members.

Last but not the least, I would like to thank all those who helped and supported me in completing my research work.

POOJA YADAV
Research Scholar
RS No. 312/15

Date:
Place: Jaipur

Preface

Stress is caused by an imbalance between the demands upon an individual and the ability to cope with those demands. The demands are perceived as challenges which may arise from either external or internal sources. Individuals have their own personal beliefs that influence their attitudes and actions against such perceived or real threats. In other words, it is apparent that individuals differ from each other in their responses to stressful events in their lives.

Organizational stressors are factors in the workplace that can cause stress. The four general sets of organizational stressors are task demands, physical demands, role demands and interpersonal demands. Stress-related problems include mood disturbance, psychological distress, sleep disturbance, upset stomach, headache, and problems in relationships with family and friends. The effects of job stress on chronic diseases are more difficult to ascertain because chronic diseases develop over a relatively long period of time and are influenced by many factors other than stress. Nonetheless, there is some evidence that stress plays a role in the development of several types of chronic health problems including cardiovascular disease, musculoskeletal disorders, and psychological disorders.

Banks are considered to be the nerve centre of an economy and the barometer of its economic perspective. The Indian banking structure consists of a heterogeneous mix of indigenous banks, the public sector and private sector commercial banks, new generation banks, foreign banks at base layers, the highly developed State Bank of India at its middle layer, and the State-owned Central Bank 'The Reserve Bank of India' at the apex.

Liberalization, deregulation and global integration of banking activities have increased the risk of the banking industry. Now banks are proactively devising their internal mechanism to withstand these risks. Banks are now rationalizing their branch network by shifting, merging, and closing down the non-viable branches. They have introduced mass computerization with the twin objectives of handling the increased volume of business effectively on the one hand, and improving the housekeeping and customer services on the other. Nationalized banks introduced the scheme of voluntary retirement to manage the surplus manpower left due to computerization. Now banks are facing severe competition. They are rationalizing the interest rate and service charges, on the one hand and becoming more customer-oriented on the other. The increasing competition and shrinking profit margin have led to the voluntary merger of the banks for gaining competitive edge. Banker-customer contact is reduced to the bare minimum and much of the business is taken over by electronic banking, tele-banking and card banking. It can be called 'Anywhere-Anytime Banking'. Banks have become the delivery channel for a host of financial products and services like the insurance, hire purchase and leasing, brokering and consultancy.

As a result of all these changes in the banking industry, life in the organization has become highly stressful. Stress leads to physical disorders because the internal body system changes while trying to cope with stress.

Stress over a long period of time leads to diseases of heart and other parts of the body. Therefore, it is important that stress, both on and off the job, must be kept at a low level so that most people may be able to handle stress without developing either emotional or physical disorders.

Thus, the study is taken up to explore *"Job Stress Among Employees of Banking Industry (A Comparative Study of Selected Public and Private Sector Banks in Haryana)"* with following set of research objectives:

- To study and compare the level of job stress among the employees of public and private sector banks.
- Exploration of various factors which have the potential to produce/cause stress.
- To compare the level of job stress experienced by male and female employees in the banks under study.
- To study the effects of stress on employee job satisfaction.
- To analyse the effects of stress on the health of employees.
- To identify and compare the various stress coping methods used by public and private sector banks.

The data were used to prove the appropriate hypothesis with the support of standard Statistical tests. The findings gave few interesting information about the employee stress level and productivity in selected banks under study.

The results showed that there was a very less difference between the means in both private and public sector banks. This shows that the level of stress in both the private and the public sector banks was almost same but public sector banks are more affected with job stress due to their comparatively low pace for adapting to the new technology and trends as well as coming up with new policies. Moreover, the public sector banks are more centralized in the sense that they are not involving their employees in decision making process as well as the communication gaps are too much. Keeping in mind these findings, the researcher concluded that main hypothesis H_1 which is "there is a significant difference between the level of stress experienced by the employees of public and private sector banks" have supported.

This research endeavor is divided into *five* chapters. *First chapter* is the introduction of the study. It presents the conceptual introduction of Job Stress as well as correlated parameters for the same. This chapter also elaborates stress management strategies followed in varied public and private sector banks for coping with job stress among employees. Public and Private sector banks employees also illustrated the impact of these coping strategies on their stress and job performance in banks.

Second chapter deals with the brief of the profile of banking sector and selected public and private sector banks under study in the study state Haryana.

Chapter three is Research methodology of the study and enlists a detailed review of literature subdivided into various categories which finally leads to the research gap of the study. To cope with the research gap this chapter contains the objectives of the study, scope of the study, hypothesis of the study, relevance and research design of the study.

Fourth chapter elaborates the data analysis, interpretation and hypothesis testing of the current research design. Chapter illustrated the empirical interpretation of all the data and also statistically examined the hypothesis under study. Finally, the significant figures have been illustrated in order to identify the statistical findings of the research.

Last, but not least *The fifth Chapter* consist of the final summary of findings, conclusion, suggestions and the scope for further study.

Thesis has supporting annexure including bibliography which is subdivided into books, journal articles, webliography, questionnaires, researchers publications and a brief profile of the researcher.

TABLE OF CONTENTS

LIST OF TABLES

LIST OF CHARTS

LIST OF FIGURES

CHAPTER-I

CONCEPTUAL INTRODUCTION

1.1 INTRODUCTION

The human resource which includes manpower is the most important and sophisticated tool of an organization under which the functionality moves in a more pragmatic and systematic manner. Without the support of human capitalization, technological advancement alone cannot provide a better quality of products and services because such advanced technology also requires the human asset to operate, that results in optimizing the utilization of resources. It can be said that the success of any organization is largely dependent on the teamwork, their competency, capability, and attitude towards the work. Less employee turnover is directly related to a positive response for any organization. Retention of the skilled workforce is like an investment for the businesses in any organization.

The banking sector is the backbone and plays a very crucial role in the growth and development of an economy. In India, the banking sector is heterogeneous in nature such as the combination of the public sector and private sector bank. However, there are some other financial institutes which are also part of the banking sector.

The concept of liberalization, deregulation and global integration and presence of banking activities have increased the risk of the banking industry. The banks nowadays are spreading as well as rationalizing its branches at a broader level by adopting the trend of emerging, amalgamating and shifting. The technological development is helping the banks in two means, the volume of business is increased and the service to the customer is improving. Various schemes like voluntary retirement have been introduced by the nationalized banks to manage the manpower which is increasing as the digital period has arrived. Because of the computerized services, banks are now facing the problem of server. By mitigating the interest rate and other charges, the banks are becoming more customer-centric by providing digital services to get a competitive advantage. Now, many banks are merging because of increasing competition. The banker-customer contact is mitigated and has become limited because of the e-services provided by the banks, being the e-service, a person can use it anytime, anywhere.

1

To maintain the pace in the modern era where growth and development and the up gradation of high technology is taking place, good and highly competitive environment of work is required, and to fulfill these needs and expectations this sector demands skilled workforce and intellect human capital to reach the aspiration of the customers. But the main problem associated with the banks is that they are not providing sufficient training to their employees to uplift their capability and competency towards work.

In the banking sector, such transformation has impacted the social, economic and psychological behavior of employees and their relations. There is already a certain level of stress in banking employees work life and then encounter even more stress arising from the work pressure that banking employees face on the job. Many employees cannot cope with such rapid changes taking place in their jobs. Role conflict, service for the customer, contribution, rapid technological change, lack of customer response is the great transaction of stress for the banking workers. It is important for any organization to keep the employee happy so that the working does not get affected and the organizational goal can be achieved efficiently and effectively. Taking these points into consideration this study is based on their stress-related problems, its consequences and various strategies to overcome with such problem of employees in the banking sector.

1.2 CONCEPT OF STRESS

The study of Stress has become one of the most crucial and important for any organization. The stress which affects the employee indirectly affects the organization as well. Thus, it can be said that stress affects the health of an individual as well as the organization as a whole. There are multiple theories which explain the term STRESS. The general acceptance, however, is that the main reason for the stress in an individual is because of the environment in which he is working/living. Thus, the study of stress in an organization can be understood as follows:

2

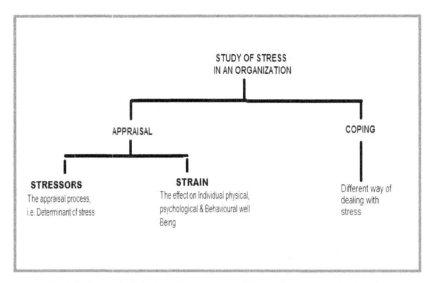

Fig 1.1. Appraisal and coping pattern of Stress in an organization.*
*Source: *Gopika G, http://www.ijarse.com, Vol. No.3, Issue No.12, December 2014*

From the above figure (Fig. 1.1), it can be interpreted that the study of stress in any organization can be based on two major aspects, viz. Appraisal and Coping. The Appraisal thereafter is further divided into two studies as the determinant of stress known as 'Stressor' and as the effect of these determinants on individuals physical, psychological and behavioral well being called 'Strain'. Coping is the study of various methods and strategies to deal with stress.

ORIGIN OF THE CONCEPT

Stress can be defined as an unusual cause of emotional feeling when people feel insecure and are in the pressure of some work. Physiological, behavioral and cognitive changes can be observed when a person is in stress. Because of its versatile nature, the concept of stress has proven to be an inaccurate term for scientific research. Stress has been made operational in many ways; and as such, it is often confused with depression, fear, lack of social support, type A behavior, hostility, and anger. Although a consensus on the definition of stress has not been reached, a generally accepted conceptualization of stress is that it is a response to a threat or challenge to the environment that exists in a continuum between excitement and fear and that is normally perceived as stress or negative effect.

Research on stress has come a long way from its earlier origins as a technical term, that is then used in research with human factors. Originally, stress was considered primarily as a physical trauma to which people reacted. More recently, it has been linked to physical events, as well as to the evaluation of events, which is a cognitive phenomenon.

The term stress is derived from the Latin word"Stringer", which means to draw tight. It was first used in the 17th century to explain and describe the hardships or afflictions. There are various definitions given in the literature for stress. Hans Selye, the father of stress, defines stress as "the non-specific response of the body to any demand for change". Moorhead and Griffin (1998) define stress as "a person's adaptive response to a stimulus that places excessive psychological or physical demands on that person." Luthans (1988) in his words defines work stress as "an adaptive response to an external situation that results in physical, psychological and behavioral deviations for organizational participants."

From the above two definitions, it can be understood that 'individuals respond in different ways when subjected to certain stressors'. The concept of stressor means the happening or creation of any fear in the mind of an individual. Physical stressors include conditions such as environmental pollution, environmental pressure such as severe temperature changes, electric shocks, prolonged exercise, injuries, other body trauma and exposure to disease. Psychological stressors refer to threats that are attributed to the internal interaction of an individual, such as thoughts, feelings, and fears about these threats. The psycho-social stressors are those that result from the interpersonal interactions, such as with colleagues at work or social isolation.

There are many definitions, models and theories about how individuals are affected by stress in the workplace. In particular, the study of psychology and stress has led to a wide range of definitions that are not all useful in clarifying the meaning of the term (Jones and Bright, 2001). After extensive literature research, Cox (1985) defines stress as, "a complex psychological condition resulting from the cognitive assessment of the person adapting to the needs of the work environment."

According to Sharit and Salvendy (1982), stress can be divided into physiological, psychological and social types that integrate the concept of coping strategies. They recognized the problem of defining stress as a stimulus or as an

4

answer. They also hypothesized that the extent to which an event is stressful depends on a complex interaction of factors including genetic predisposition, early social experience, cultural factors, and a life conditioning process.

According to Kroemer et al. (2001) the three major aspects of Stress are:

1. The demand for the job, which depends on the work, the environment of the work and conditions of the work, are considered to be the job stressors.

2. The capabilities of a person to fulfill the requirement of the job.

3. The attitude of an individual, which must match with the demands of the job.

The exemplary stressful circumstance is one in which the individual's resources are not well coordinated to the level of interest and where there are constraints in coping, and minimal social help. Mc Grawth (1970) has given a most accepted and acknowledged meaning of stress: "a perceived, substantial imbalance between demand and response capability, under conditions where failure to meet the demand has important perceived consequences".

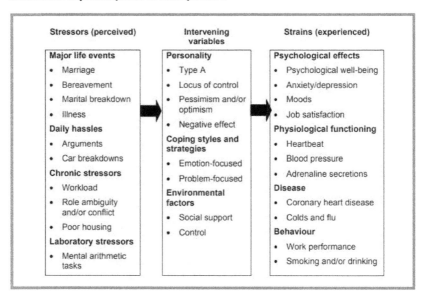

Fig. 1.2. The factors of stress Framework*

*Source: *Mc Grawth (1970)*

1.3 JOB STRESS

Nowadays the phenomenon of work consumes a large extent of employees lives. Value of work in the lives of people can be a source of more stress. The main reason for job stress is people having long working hours, fear of losing the job, upgradation in technologies or the increasing burden on employees due to change in the working environment. All these have an effect on the personal lives of people which makes their work more difficult. There are many sources of stress which occur every day in an individual's life and most of them report stress to some extent. In the life of an individual, problems related with occupation can be the major cause of stress. It can happen due to various reasons such as close intervention and interference, more working hours, noise pollution, or dealing with lethal goods.

Job stress is a serious and enduring problem in the workplace. The last few decades have brought about dramatic changes in the nature of work in organizations. Job stress can be defined as the physiological and emotional responses that occur when workers perceive an imbalance between their work demands and their capability and/or resources to meet these demands (NIOSH, 1999).

As per Newman (1979), job stress is "a condition arising out of the interaction of people with their jobs and characterizes by changes within people that forces them to drift apart from normal functioning."

1.4 TYPES OF STRESS/VARIATIONS OF STRESS:

1.4.1EUSTRESS

The term eustress means positive or favorable stress and it can be either physical, psychological, biochemical or radiological.

It was first introduced by Endocrinologist Hans Selye consisting of the prefix "eu" which means good. So it is a type of strain or pressure which means good stress.

Richard Lazarus explored this stress in a stress model. It is a positive response of your cognitive skill and so it is treated as healthy stress, or it gives you a feeling of fulfillment or other positive feelings. Hans introduced this term as a stress subgroup to differ the wide variety of stressors and manifestations of stress.

Eustress is not defined by the stressor type, but instead how one perceives that stressor e.g. a negative fear against a positive challenge. Eustress is the positive response that one has to a stressor and it can be dependent on one's feeling of desire, control, location or timing of the stressor. When any stress gives the strength of hope, optimistic vision or any meaningful sense then it is termed as eustress. Eustress has a positive correlation with life satisfaction and well-being. Eustress is not comfortable but it plays an important role in the personal growth of an individual.

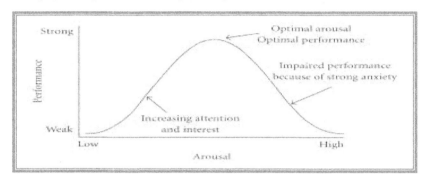

Fig. 1.3 Yerkes–Dodson curve for a difficult task*

***Source:** Yerkes RM, Dodson JD (1908). "The relation of strength of stimulus to rapidity of habit-formation". Journal of Comparative Neurology and Psychology*

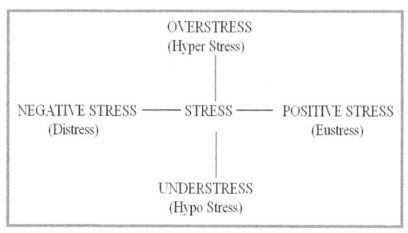

Fig 1.4 Four Variations of Stress*

***Source:** Rita Agarwal (2005). Stress in life and at work. New Delhi: Response Books.*

1.4.2 DISTRESS:

Another important variation of stress is distress which has negativity in its characteristic. Distress is a threat to the quality of life. It leads the path of human's life towards anxiety, tension, and depression. It occurs when a demand vastly exceeds a person's capabilities. This can also happen when social trauma occurs such as in the case of the black death and during the time of world war 2 which was the reason for the great distress.

This negative stress is brought by fixed readjustment and to find the alternatives in daily life. It gives birth to negative feelings. Distress can be of two types i.e., acute stress and chronic stress. Acute stress is deep stress that comes and goes immediately and chronic stress is long-time stress that is for weeks, months, or years. Both acute stress and chronic stress can result in a negative impact on one's health physically, mentally and emotionally. It is very crucial to recognize such type of stress as catastrophic and recognize the ways to minimize and manage such emotions.

1.4.3 HYPER STRESS:

Hyper stress occurs at that moment when an individual is forced beyond his/her capability and it results from an individual being overloaded or overworked. In such situations, even small things can trigger an individual's strong emotional response.

Hyper stress has an adverse impact on the health of an individual both in the short term as well as in the long term. All the phases of a person's life are likely to be affected by hyper stress which includes their work life, home life, social life, and personal relationships.

1.4.4 HYPO STRESS:

Hypo stress is the opposite of hyper stress. It occurs when an individual is fed up or do not have any challenge and it usually happens with the repetition of the same works. An individual who suffers from hypo stress generally does not have inspiration and new things to do. A worker in any firm who is doing the same task on a daily basis can suffer from hypo stress.

While this type of stress is not generally considered harmful in the short term, it can have significant negative impacts over the long term, affecting a person's motivation, performance, and overall health and wellbeing.

1.5 MODELS OF STRESS

Under any study, a model plays a very important role in presenting a historical picture of the phenomenon. A model of stress also enables a visual image of the phenomenon in its totality which includes the causal factors, the symptoms, the process, and the result.

Several models and theories have been used in the literature to explain and analyze the phenomenon of workplace stress. The theories include various models such as Selye's General Adaptation Syndrome (Selye, 1976), Canon's work that underlies Selye's proposition (Canon, 1935) and Lazarus transactional model of stress (Lazarus, 1966).

A number of models have been presented over the years, starting from the models analyzing only one side to those trying to supply a general framework for the understanding of the strain development. The models that have dominated the literature on stress are reviewed as below:

1.5.1. RESPONSE BASED MODEL

In this theoretical model, stress has been interpreted as a response from the individual. As a response, the definition of Stress is given by Selye as "A non-specific response of the body to any type of application that is applied to it". Selye's model is popularly known as General Adaptation Syndrome (GAS). The term "stressor" was introduced by Selye for differentiating stress causes and the response to this, with a motive that each factor can cause the stress and influence the balance of the individual. Selye mentioned as the stress is an inner part of the body, the responses can be changed and observed by this. This syndrome of general adjustment of the body's reaction (GAS) is showed by discharging a few hormones, which have prompted changes in the structure and chemical composition of the body. Notwithstanding the adjustment of the entire body, an incomplete response of the body or an organ is conceivable. This reaction to push is called Local Adaption Syndrome (LAS).

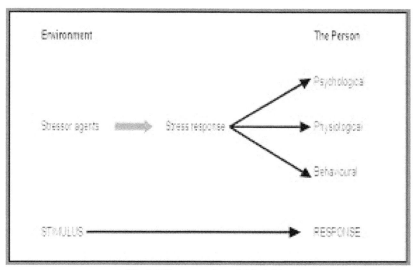

Fig.1.5 Response based Model *
*Source: Sutherland and Cooper(2010)

1.5.2 PERSON-ENVIRONMENT (P-E) FIT MODEL

The person-environment fit model is the degree of adjustment or coincidence between you and your work environment. The theory behind the person-environment adjustment is that everyone has a work environment with which they are more compatible. The idea of PE is based on Kurt Lewin's maxim according to which behavior is a function of the person and the environment. The characteristics of the person's side of the equation include interests, preferences, KSA (knowledge, skills, and abilities), personality traits, values, and objectives. Environmental factors may include aspects such as professional standards, work requirements, job characteristics, and the organization's culture and values. The basic foundation of the theory is simple: if you work in an optimal compatible environment, all kinds of good things happen, such as a better attitude to work, performance, and less stress.

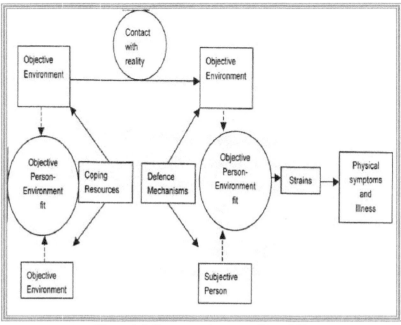

Figure 1.6: Person-environment fit model*
*Source: *Harrison, 1978*

1.5.3 THE JOB DEMAND/DECISION LATITUDE MODEL

The belief that work-related stress has an adverse effect on health is widely accepted by the general public and several constructs have been developed to explain how the work and the work environment interacts to increase the stress. The most used models are the Karasek-Theorell work registration model, whose two core components are high work demands (the need to work fast and hard) and low latitude decision making (lack of control over the use of skills, temporary allocation, and organizational decisions). The theory states that workers who have a concurrent latitude and high decision-making needs cannot moderate the stress caused by high demands by managing time or learning new skills, and therefore are subject to high stress at work and they are at greater risk of the disease. Therefore, there are limitations in the decision-making process, along with the high demands that produce the unhealthy condition of "stress at work". The Job Demand model was initially used to explain the patterns of depression, burnout and job dissatisfaction, but then it was extended to include cardiovascular disease (examined by Schnall and Hemingway), malfunctioning of health and absenteeism. As the literature has accumulated, the model has been refined. The model of iso-information affirms that the workload is particularly harmful to people with a low level of social assistance in the workplace since social networks can cushion the effects of forced labor.

Similarly, high incomes and the availability of tangible resources can reduce the effect of work stress on health, so that stress could be more damaging among workers with low socio-economic status (SES) and in younger age groups.

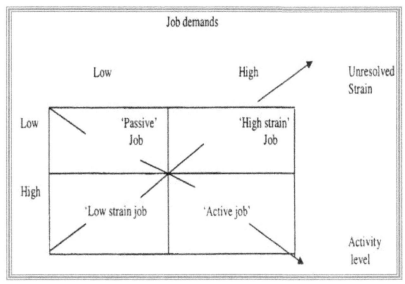

Figure 1.7: Karasek's demand-control Model*
***Source:** Karasek R, D (1962)*

1.5.4. STIMULUS BASED MODEL

In the stimulus-based model, the stress is viewed as an independent factor, whereas in the response-based model it is not, and this is the difference between the two. The Environment is considered as the disturbing factor in STIMULUS BASED MODEL. As per the nature and perspective of an individual, there are different points of view and opinions of the same happening and this could be a reason for stress.

People are able to face and tolerate the stress to an extent but once this level exceeds the tolerance limit, there may be some damage like physiological, behavioral or psychological.

Based on this model, the main objective of the research is to recognize the reasons and sources of the stress in the work environment. The figure of Stimulus Based Model is given below.

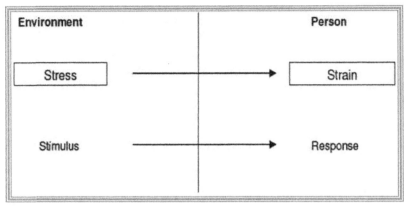

Fig.1.8 Stimulus-based model of stress.

1.5.5 TRANSACTIONAL MODELS OF STRESS

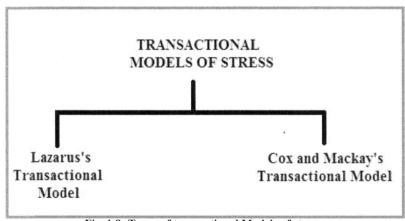

Fig. 1.9: Types of transactional Models of stress.

13

1.5.5.1 Lazarus's transactional model

This model is a psychological based model in which there is a transaction/interaction between the individual and the work. Stress according to this model occurs because of an imbalance between demand and the resources. It implies that when the pressure to work is more than that of the ability to cope and mediate stress, an individual becomes stressed. The characteristics of situations are not considered in this approach. The figure of the model is given below.

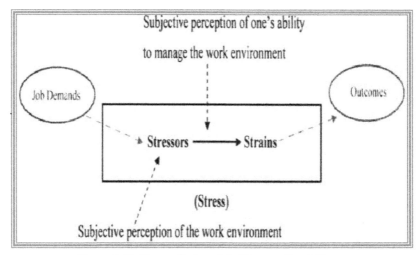

Figure 1.10: Theoretical model of Occupational Stress

1.5.5.2 Cox and Mackay's transactional model of stress

This model is a comprehension of the multiple components which are considered to analyze the stress level. The factors which are included in this approach are:

- Perception of demand and capacity

- Emotional and stress response

- Physiological and psychological response

- Behavioral and cognitive response

- Comments on the evaluation response

1.6 SYMPTOMS OF STRESS

Nowadays, stress is a disease and it has become an integral part of human life. The nature and severity of stress can be properly and conveniently understood by observing the various symptoms which occur in the employee under the conditions of job stress. Beehr and Newman 1978, categorized the symptoms of stress as psychological, physical and behavioral. These symptoms are discussed below:

1.6.1 Psychological Symptoms:

Psychological stress occurs due to anxiety, tension, boredom, helplessness, depression, insecurity, isolation, etc. Psychological symptoms of stress also include job-dissatisfaction, frustration, dislike for the job and resentment. The psychological symptoms of stress are difficult to identify, until and unless the suffered person does not tell about his/her stress. The reason being, it is an internal process or phenomenon which gets affected by the influence of mind while dealing with the situations based on different criteria in daily life.

1.6.2 Physical Symptoms:

Numerous physical symptoms that commonly occur before the onset of a serious illness related to stress, have been identified by various researchers. These include cardiovascular diseases, gastrointestinal problems, allergies and skin diseases, headaches, nervous contractions, hypertension, indigestion, and respiratory diseases.

1.6.3 Behavioral Symptoms:

Behavioral symptoms are easily observable and are classified into two categories as employee-centered symptoms and organization related symptoms. The employee-centered symptoms include avoidance of work, increased consumption of alcohol or drugs, change in appetite, aggression towards coworkers or family members, etc. The organization related symptoms include absenteeism, low job involvement, low performance, accident proneness, loss of responsibility, reduced creativity, etc.

1.7 SOURCES OF STRESS

According to Cooper (1986), stress is observed as the product of an interaction between individual needs and resources and the various demands, constraints, and facilitators within the individual's immediate environment. Different factors cause stress in different people. The various causes or sources of stress can be classified into four broad categories: - Extra-organizational, Organizational, Individual and Group.

1.7.1 Extra-organizational Stressors: Extra-organizational sources are the factors outside the organization that causes stress. These are the environmental factors of stress which precipitate the stress response in an individual, but which originate outside the individual. These include fast technological changes, social changes, economic conditions, ethnic identity, political changes, relocation and transfers, financial difficulties, family issues, life events, etc.

1.7.2 Organizational Stressors: Stressors exist not only outside the organization but also within it. Organization Stressors are those which are beyond the control of an individual at the workplace and this result in frustration. The various types of Stressors operating at work are explained as follows:

1.7.2.1 Factors intrinsic to the job: It includes all those sources of stress which are integrally connected to the particular job requirements for each job. Stress can arise from too much or too little work. The major sources of stress identified under this category include the following:

- Improper working conditions

- Work overload or under load

- Technological advancement

- Information overload

- Organizational tasks

- Time pressure

- Excessive travel

- Long hours of work

1.7.2.2 Role in the Organization: A role at the workplace is another cause of stress in people at work. An individual has to perform different roles both at home and at the workplace. At home the individual has to perform the role of father, husband, etc. and at the workplace a role of boss, subordinate or team leader, etc. Performing all these roles simultaneously causes anxiety and stress. The various sources of stress in an organizational role include role ambiguity, role conflict, etc. Pareek (1983) pioneered work on role stress by identifying the following role stressors:

- Inter-Role Distance (IRD)

- Role Stagnation (RS)

- Self-Role Distance (SRD)

- Role Ambiguity (RA)

- Role Expectation Conflict (REC)

- Role Overload (RO)

- Role Erosion (RE)

- Role Inadequacy (RIn)

- Personal Inadequacy (PI)

- Role Isolation (RI)

1.7.2.3 Relationship at Work: The nature of the relationship with others in the workplace is a major source of stress. Quality of relationship at work plays a dominant role in determining employee's job behavior and job strains. The various types of relationships identified at the workplace are the relationship with co-workers, relationship within work groups and relationship with superiors and subordinates. Poor relation at work involves low trust, low support and low interest in listening to and dealing with organizational problems of the members.

1.7.2.4 Organizational Structure and Climate: Certain features of organizational structure and climate also have the potential to cause severe psychological stress to its employees. Depending upon the extent of involvement of employees in decision making organizational structure can be of two types: centralized and decentralized. It is found that the organizations which allow the participation of employees in the workplace are less stressful than the organizations which do not. Poor organizational climate may also be a reason of stress among employees.

1.7.2.5 Career Development: Advancement in the career is the utmost important aspect for almost all the employees. Lack of job security, under promotion or over promotion, etc. may contribute to high levels of stress. The two major clusters of potential stressors that are identified in the area of career development are:

1. Lack of job security, fear of redundancy, obsolescence or early retirement.

2. Status incongruity, frustration stemming from reaching one's career ceiling.

1.7.3 Individual Stressors: Reaction to pressure at work varies from person to person. Some have better skills to overcome while others do not. Many factors contribute to this difference, such as personality, age, gender, motivation, the inability to overcome problems in the field of specialization, fluctuations in skills, etc. (Cooper and Marshal, 1978).

Various individual factors which cause stress include the following:

1.7.3.1 Life Changes: Changes in one's life and career also lead to stress. Changes occurring at a fast pace are more threatening than the slow pace changes because fast pace changes cause more stress. Heart attacks are commonly observed in the case of rapid changes in life and careers. People, who are more devoted to work, are more prone to stress than the others.

1.7.3.2 Role Perceptions: Individuals are required to perform varied roles in their organizational and personal life. While performing all these roles simultaneously he experiences stress because it is difficult to perform equally well in all the diverse roles.

1.7.3.3 Personality Type: Personality also affects behavior. Type A and Type B personalities are studied in this context. Always walking and eating rapidly, feeling impatient, hyper-alertness, the explosiveness of speech, doing several things simultaneously, etc. are some common behavioral patterns of Type A personality which is stress-prone. On the other hand, Type B personality is less stress-prone. Not concerned about time, being patient, playing for fun not to win, no pressing deadlines, never in hurry, etc. are some characteristics of Type B personality.

1.7.3.4 Low Self-esteem: People with low self-esteem usually underrate themselves and in the act of doing so they develop a negative attitude which ultimately leads to/ causes stress.

18

1.7.3.5 Age: Age also plays a dominant role in studying stress. In today's stressful environment, people at an earlier age are more stressed at the job.

1.7.4 Group Stressors: Group can also be a potential source of the stressor. Lack of group cohesiveness, lack of social support system, Interpersonal and inter-group conflict are some common group level stressors. Further, managers may create stress for employees by:

i.   Exhibiting inconsistent behaviors'.

ii. Showing a lack of concern.

iii. Providing inadequate directions & information.

iv. Providing no support.

v.   Ignoring good performance & focusing on negatives.

vi. Creating a high productivity environment.

vii. Sexual harassment.

1.8 CONSEQUENCES OF STRESS

As per Newman (1979), job stress is "a condition arising out of interaction of people with their jobs and characterizes by changes within people that forces them to drift apart from normal functioning."

Individuals have different personalities and thus, the effect of stress is different for different individuals. The various consequences of stress can be classified into the following categories:

• Consequences for the individual.

• Consequences for the organization.

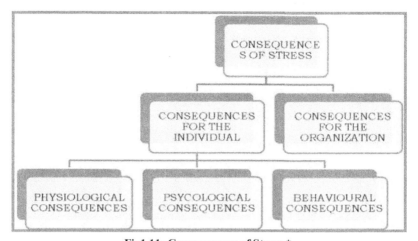

Fig1.11: Consequences of Stress.*

***Source:** Researchers understanding based on secondary data*

1.8.1 Consequences for the Individual: Stress may appear in a number of ways. The individual consequences of stress can be studied under the following three general categories:

1.8.1.1 Physiological Consequences: According to many types of research related with health and medical sciences, stress may result in massive heart attack, increased headache, increased Blood pressure, abnormal breathing, respiratory diseases, elevation in cholesterol level, etc. Stress affects the human body and is physically related to cardiovascular disease, hypertension, ulcers, asthma, and migraine headache. High physical stress causes high metabolic rate and thus affects the body glands and disrupts the body functioning.

1.8.1.2 Psychological Consequences: Psychological consequences of stress are related to an individual's emotional health and thought process. Individuals may become depressed or they may start sleeping too much or too little if too much stress is experienced by them at the workplace. Experiences of strain might lead to depression, anger, tension, boredom, fatigue, irritation, frustration, least self-actualization, accidental withdraw, feeling of ugliness, anxiety, loss of sense of humor, family problems, sexual difficulties, etc.

1.8.1.3 Behavioral Consequences: Stress affects the behavior of an individual. With a change in the stress level, the behavior of an individual also changes. Behavioral consequences of stress include accident proneness, violence, appetite disorder, depression, emotional disorder, drug abuse, increased smoking and drinking, reduction in productivity, absenteeism, and turnover. Stress affects the decision-making power of employee adversely and they may also develop a negative attitude towards their job. Stress also affects the ability to adopt new methods and processes adversely.

1.8.2 Consequences for the Organization: Stress affects not only the employees but also the organization, as a whole is affected by stress adversely. Job stress affects the organization in a number of ways, some of which are listed below:

- Increased rate of absenteeism;

- Stress reduces the motivation level of workers due to which many workers don't show up for work;

- Excessive stress may lead to increased accidents or illness and thus, a cost to company arises in the form of healthcare;

- Rate of accident goes up;

- Due to stress, there is a lack of commitment to the work;

- Productivity decreases due to low job performance;

- Increased customer complaints;

- Stress may even cause strikes and sabotage due to destructive and aggressive behavior;

- Resignation of employees from the job; and

- Stressed out employees may even take legal action against the company.

1.9 COPING WITH STRESS

Stress can have a major impact on the mental and physical health of human beings. After learning how to recognize stress and identify its resources, let's see how one can cope with it.

1.9.1 Concept of Coping

Coping refers to the thoughts and actions that are used while dealing with a threatful situation. Coping means to overcome with some certain problems or coming from one difficult situation to a good situation. Coping may be referred to as investing one's own conscious effort for solving a personal or interpersonal problem that will help in overcoming, minimizing or tolerating stress.

McGrath (1970) defined coping — "as an array of covert or overt behavior patterns by which the organism can actively prevent, alleviate, or respond to stress-inducing circumstances."

Folkman & Lazarus (1980) defined coping "as the cognitive and behavioral efforts made to master, tolerate or reduce external and internal demands and conflicts among them which tax or exceed a person's resources."

Coping usually takes place to handle the situations, which are perceived to be harmful, threatening or challenging. The efficacy of the coping effort hinge's on the type of stress, the individual and the situation. Coping responses are partly governed by habitual traits i.e. personality, and partly by the social environment.

1.9.2 Types of Coping Strategies

Individuals, as well as organizations, cannot be in tension for a long time. They have to adopt some strategies so that they can overcome stress. These strategies are called coping strategies. There are two connections of the word coping with stress literature. Either it has been used to denote the way of dealing with stress, or the effort to 'master' the conditions that are harmful, threatening or challenging when a routine or automatic response is not readily available.

The coping process in its broadest sense refers to any attempt to deal with a stressful situation which a person feels he must do something about, but which taxes or exceeds his existing adaption response patterns.

Schwarzer(2000), identified four types of coping:

- **Reactive coping:** an effort to deal with a stressful event which has already occurred.

- **Anticipatory coping:** an effort to deal with an impending threat or a stressful event which is likely to occur in the near future.

- **Preventive coping:** efforts taken to minimize the likelihood of experiencing, or reducing the impact of stress in the future.

- **Proactive coping:** a process of identifying the potential stressors and then acting in advance either to avert them or to reduce or minimize their effect.

1.9.3. INDIVIDUAL COPING STRATEGIES

TABLE 1.1 INDIVIDUAL COPING STRATEGIES

COGNITIVE	PHYSICAL	ENVIRONMENT	OTHER
Therapy	Artistic Expression	Music	Conflict resolution
Hobbies	Deep Breathing	Nature	Prayer
Meditation	Natural Medicine	Pets	
Mindfulness	Physical Exercise	Spa Visit	
Planning	Relaxation		
Reading	Yoga		
Time Management			

A number of individual coping strategies have been studied and are considered effective in managing work stress. Exercise, relaxation, looking after yourself, flip your negative thinking, reducing job stress by prioritizing and organizing, time management, expressing yourself, confronting the problem, social support, finding distractions, etc. are some of the commonly used individual coping strategies which are explained below:

1.9.3.1 Exercise:

Exercise can be an effective component of a stress management program and all types of exercises can be used for stress management. Training programs consistent with current recommendations can be prescribed to improve health to manage stress. Fitness professionals should recognize that it may be necessary to direct a client to a psychologist or other health care professional to help develop strategies to control stressors that produce chronic acute episodic stress.

1.9.3.2 Relaxation:

When we think about the ideals of relaxation, an image of a solitary monk in a temple with bells in the background comes into the mind. It has been said that a permanent devotion to inner peace would be ideal for relieving stress, but for now, aiming a little more realistically with some simple methods, it could better fit an individual's daily routine and be easier to maintain in the long run.

As a general rule, relaxation techniques involve diverting attention from what makes an individual feel anxious, scared or stressed and focusing on something that calms him/her down. While the type of relationship method an individual chooses is important, it is more important to engage in regular, focused practice and mastering your technique.

1.9.3.3 Looking After Yourself:

According to this strategy, one should be kind to himself/herself and should take proper breaks during the work period. One should give himself/herself "me time" in which he/she can do whatever they want to such as taking rest, getting a massage, doing yoga or meditation, spending time with family and friends, etc. Doing all these things will surely help in tackling stress.

1.9.3.4 Flip Your Negative Thinking:

Being/thinking negative in every situation and interaction will do you no good than just draining out your energy and motivation level. So always try to be positive about yourself and your work, and also try to avoid people with negative thoughts. You should also sometimes pat yourself on the back for your small achievements, even if no one else do's that.

1.9.3.5 Reducing Stress by Prioritizing and Organizing:

When workplace stress overwhelms you then there are some steps which you should take to regain control over yourself and the situation. In order to reduce workplace stress always try to create a balanced schedule, don't try to fit too much into one day, try to leave 10-15 minutes earlier in the morning, always take regular short breaks throughout the day, prioritize your tasks and break large projects into small steps.

1.9.3.6 Time Management:

The pressure of time is considered as the most noticeable cause of stress among the higher authorities. Hence, time management plays a very important role in reducing stress.

Luthans, (2002:415) listed some of the most helpful guidelines for effective time management:

1. Create a list of "to-dos" that identifies everything that must be done during the day. This helps keep track of work progress.

2. Delegate as little work as possible to subordinates.

3. Determine when to do the best job, morning or afternoon, and plan the most difficult task for this period of time.

4. Spend time during the day, preferably at least one hour, when visits or other interruptions can be avoided.

5. Voicemail all incoming calls to eliminate those that are minor or do not require your personal attention.

6. Eat lunch in the office one or two days a week to save time and have the opportunity to resume paperwork.

7. Discourage visitors who stay in the room by turning your desk to avoid looking at the door or hallway.

8. Read standing. The average person reads faster and more accurately when in a slightly uncomfortable position.

9. Make phone calls between 4:30 and 5:00 p.m. People tend to keep their conversation short at this time so that they can go home early.

10. Do not feel guilty about those things that have not been done today. Put them at the top of the task list for tomorrow.

1.9.3.7 Express Yourself:

Expressing your feelings to others can help a great deal in relieving stress. Sometimes crying or even striking or beating a pillow can calm your feelings of anxiety and thus reduce stress.

1.9.3.8 Confront the Problem:

Always try to face the situation rather than ignoring it or running away from it. Instead of letting things go when someone is rude to you or when something according to you is wrong, you should confront them. Confronting the problem or situation will decrease the stress and increase efficiency and productivity and improve the working environment.

1.9.3.9 Social Support:

Social support from friends, family members, professionals, and other key contributors will be a key factor in reducing stress in the workplace. Such support does not reduce your self-esteem when you do this by applying your wisdom. There are a number of studies showing the positive effects of a strong support network on physical and mental health. Strong and deep relationships with others guarantee timely help in difficult times. Stroebe (in Forshaw 2002:66) has outlined the main categories of social support which include appraisal support, emotional support, esteem support, information support, and instrumental support.

1.9.3.10 Find Distractions:

Indulge yourself into some sports and physical activities like walking, swimming, jogging, cycling, etc. This will help you in reducing both mental and physical stress. Even talking to other people can also help in reducing your stress levels.

1.10 STRESS MANAGEMENT

Today workplace stress is becoming a matter of concern for all the organizations. The banking sector is no more an exception. Workplace stress has emerged as the black plague in this present scenario. In India, banks are amongst the top ten stressed workplaces. Despite feeling relaxed with the advent of modern technology and innovations in the banking sector, employees are feeling overloaded with work and stressed out. With the advancement in technology, banks have to make rapid changes. It has become hard for employees to cope with these changes. And the result is stress.

Various studies have depicted that stress is increasing at a rising rate in the banking sector. Due to the recession in the global market and cut-throat competition, banks are facing many challenges. As a response to which, they have to make efforts to increase their efficiency. Banks, these days, are restructuring themselves. This results in more workload on their employees. Organization stress ultimately results in employee turnover, changes in employees behavior and attitude. A little banking stress is healthy as it increases efficiency. But stress beyond limits destroys the inner peace of the employees working in banks and ultimately hampers the growth of the individual as well as the banks *(Mahalakshmi and P. Jeyasri, 2015)*.

With the rising problem of stress, stress management has become very important. Stress Management refers to the wide range of techniques and psychotherapies which can prevent and control an individual's level of stress. Thereby, improving everyday functioning of an individual. Stress management can have any of the three solutions – prevent or control, escape from it, or learn to adapt to it. As it is said that prevention is better than cure, steps should be taken at the initial stage to prevent the stressors rather than curing its harmful effects or bearing heavy costs after being affected by it. Effective stress management can be done at the individual level as well as at the banking level in various ways. Stress management can be divided into two phases: the first is coping with stress and the second is facing the stress with the help of relaxation techniques such as meditation. As every individual is different, psychotherapies should be used. Banks should treat people at work differently. Banks should introduce "Employee Assistance Programmes" (EAP) and stress control workshops according to the level of employees as the level of stress and employees are directly related. If psychological wellness and health of the employees are improved, productivity shall also increase, because it is said that, *"A Healthy Employee is a Productive Employee"*.

Many bank employees are finding it harder than ever to cope with stress in the workplace. Regardless of occupation, seniority or salary level, they are spending more and more of their workdays feeling frazzled and out of control, instead of alert and relaxed.

While some stress is a normal part of the workplace, excessive stress can interfere with productivity and reduce physical and emotional health. Finding ways to manage workplace stress is not about making huge changes to every aspect of the work life or rethinking career ambitions. Rather, stress management requires to focus on the one thing which is always within one's control.

Stressful situations in banks are real and inevitable. It is not feasible to eliminate stress totally from the work (*Xavior Selvakumar & S. Lawrence Immanuel, 2015*). Thus, there is a need to manage stress. Stress that is effectively managed by an individual is a positive symptom and requires the knowledge of "stress coping techniques" for reducing or providing an outlet to stress.

1.10.1 BANKING STRESS MANAGEMENT STRATEGIES

While the previous approaches are geared to help the individuals to cope with stress, stress management by the banking sector is designed to reduce the harmful effects of stress in two ways.

(a) Institutional Programmes

Institutional programmes to manage stress are undertaken through established organizational mechanisms. Properly designed job and work schedules can help to reduce stress. So, the design of work and work schedules should be a focus of management efforts to reduce stress. The bank's culture can also be used to help manage stress. Consider that in some banks, there is a strong norm against ever taking time off or going on vacation. In the long run, such a norm can cause major stress (*E Gordon & K. Natrajan*). Thus, the banking sector should strive to foster a culture that reinforces a healthy mix of work and no work activities.

(b) Collateral Programmes

A collateral stress programme is a managerial programme specifically created to help employees deal with stress and organizations have adopted stress management programmes, health promotion programmes and other kinds of programmes also.

1.10.1.1 UNHEALTHY WAYS OF MANAGING STRESS

These coping strategies may temporarily reduce stress, but they cause more damage in the long run:

- Smoking

- Drinking too much

- Overeating or underrating

- Zoning out for hours in front of the TV or computer

- Withdrawing from friends, family, and activities

28

- Using pills or drugs to relax

- Sleeping too much

- Procrastinating

- Filling up every minute of the day to avoid facing problems

- Taking out one's stress on others (lashing out, angry outbursts, physical violence)

1.10.1.2 HEALTHY WAYS OF MANAGING STRESS

Since everyone has a unique response to stress, there is no — "one size fits all" solution to managing it. No single method works for everyone or in every situation, so experiment with different techniques and strategies *(Awan K. 2012)*.

- **Set aside relaxation time:** One should include rest and relaxation in the daily schedule. One should not allow other obligations to encroach. The activities discussed below will help one to a great extent in attaining relaxation.

- **Connect with others:** Spending time with positive people who enhance life will provide a strong support system which will buffer one from the negative effects of stress.

- **Do something to enjoy every day:** Make time for leisure activities that bring joy, whether it be stargazing, playing the piano, or working on a bike.

- **Keep the sense of humor:** This includes the ability to laugh at our self. The act of laughing helps one's body to fight stress in a number of ways.

- **Exercise regularly:** Physical activity plays a key role in reducing and preventing the effects of stress. Make time for at least 30 minutes of exercise, three times per week. Nothing beats aerobic exercise for releasing pent-up stress and tension.

- **Eat a healthy diet:** Well-nourished bodies are better prepared to cope with stress, so one should be mindful of what he eats. Start a day right with breakfast and keep energy up and the mind clear with balanced, nutritious meals throughout the day

- **Reduce caffeine and sugar:** The temporary "highs" caffeine and sugar provide often end in with a crash in mood and energy. By reducing the amount of coffee, soft drinks, chocolate and sugar snacks in diet, one will feel more relaxed and sleep better.

- **Avoid alcohol, cigarettes, and drugs:** Self-medicating with alcohol or drugs may provide an easy escape from stress, but the relief is only temporary. Do not avoid or mask the issue at hand; deal with problems head-on and with a clear mind.

- **Get enough sleep:** Adequate sleep fuels one's mind, as well as body. Feeling tired will increase stress because it may cause one to think irrationally.

1.10.1.3 STRESS MANAGEMENT STRATEGIES: THE FOUR A's

Change the situation:	**Change the reaction:**
1. Avoid the stressor.	1. Adapt to the stressor.
2. Alter the stressor.	2. Accept the stressor.

Strategy 1: Avoid the stressor

Not all stress can be avoided and it's not healthy to avoid a situation that needs to be addressed *(Banerjee, Amalesh and Shrawan, 2001)*. One may be surprised, however, by the number of stressors in life that one can eliminate.

- **Learning to say "no"** – Know the limits and stick to them. Whether in personal or professional life, one should refuse to accept added responsibilities when they are close to reaching them. Taking on more than one can handle is a surefire recipe for stress.

- **Avoid people who stress you out** – If someone consistently causes stress in life and one cannot turn the relationship around, then limiting the amount of time spent with that person or ending the relationship entirely will help to a great extent.

- **Take control of the environment** – One should learn to take control of the environment by finding out the alternative ways.

- **Avoid hot-button topics** – If one gets upset over religion or politics, cross them off the conversation list. If one repeatedly argues about the same subject with the same people, stop bringing it up or excuse when it's the topic of discussion.

- **Pare down the to-do list** – Analyze the schedule, responsibilities and daily tasks. If there is too much on the plate, distinguish between the —"shoulds" and the —"musts". One should drop tasks that aren't truly necessary to the bottom of the list or eliminate them entirely.

Strategy 2: Alter the stressor

One should try to avoid a stressful situation & figure out what can be done to change things so that the problem does not present itself in the future. Often, this involves changing the way to communicate and operate in one's daily life.

- **Express the feelings instead of bottling them up** - If something or someone is bothering one, communicate the concerns in an open and respectful way. If an employee does not voice his feelings, resentment will build and the situation will likely remain the same *(Deepak Chawala & Neena Sondhi, 2014)*.

- **Be willing to compromise** - When one asks someone to change the behaviour, anyone should be willing to do the same. If both are willing to bend at least a little, they have a good chance of finding a happy middle ground.

- **Be more assertive** - One should not take a backseat in life. Dealing with problems head-on, doing the best to anticipate and prevent them will give a great amount of confidence.

- **Manage the time better** - Poor time management can cause a lot of stress. When one is stretched too thin and running behind, it's hard to stay calm and focused. But if an employee plans ahead and makes sure that he does not overextend himself, then this can alter the amount of stress the employee may suffer.

Strategy 3: Adapt to the stressor

If one cannot change the stressor, then changing oneself is the best solution. One can adapt to stressful situations and regain a sense of control by changing the expectations and attitude.

- **Reframe problems** - One should try to view stressful situations from a more positive perspective. This is because every problem provides an opportunity for an individual. The opportunity can be like a chance to learn something new, create innovative ideas, try to find appropriate resources, etc.

- **Look at the big picture** - One should take perspective of the stressful situation and ask how important it will be in the long run. Will it matter in a month? A year? Is it really worth getting upset over? If the answer is no, then one should focus available time and energy elsewhere.

- **Adjust your standards** - Perfectionism is a major source of avoidable stress. One should stop setting up for failure by demanding perfection. Set reasonable standards for self and others and learn to be okay with —"good enough".

- **Focus on the positive** - When stress is getting one down, then one should take a moment to reflect on all the things to appreciate in life, including one's own positive qualities and gifts. This simple strategy can help an employee keep things in perspective.

- **Adjusting Your Attitude** - One should learn to avoid stress which can have a profound effect on your emotional and physical well-being. Each negative thought about oneself makes the body react as if it were in the thorns of a tension-filled situation *(Baladev R. Sharma, 2011)*. If one sees good things about self, then it gives a good feeling and the reverse is also true.

Strategy 4: Accept the Stressor

Some sources of stress are unavoidable. One cannot prevent or change stressors such as the death of a loved one, a serious illness, or a national recession. In such cases, the best way to cope with stress is to accept things as they are. Acceptance may be difficult, but in the long run, it's easier than railing against a situation one cannot change.

- **Do not try to control the uncontrollable** - Many things in life are beyond one's control— particularly the behavior of other people. Rather than stressing out over them, focus on the things one can control such as the way to choose to react to problems.

- **Look for the upside** - As the saying goes, —"What doesn't kill us makes us stronger". When facing major challenges, one should try to look at them as opportunities for personal growth. If one's own poor choices contributed to a stressful situation, then reflecting on them and learning from the mistakes will avoid stress in the future.

- **Share your feelings** - One should talk to a trusted friend or make an appointment with a therapist. Expressing what one is going through can be very cathartic, even if there is nothing one can do to alter the stressful situation.

- **Learn to forgive** - One should accept the fact that all live in an imperfect world and that people make mistakes. Let go of anger and resentments. People can well free themselves from negative energy by forgiving and moving on.

1.10.2 STRESS MANAGEMENT MODEL FOR BANKING SECTOR

1.10.2.1 TRANSACTIONAL MODEL

i. Richard Lazarus and Susan Folkman suggested in 1984 that stress can be thought of as resulting from an "imbalance between demands and resources" or as occurring when "pressure exceeds one's perceived ability to cope". Stress management was developed and premised on the idea that stress is not a direct response to a stressor but rather one's resources and ability to cope mediate the stress response and are amenable to change, thus allowing stress to be controllable (*Deolalkar, G.H. 2000*).

ii. In order to develop an effective stress management programme it is first necessary to identify the factors that are central to a person controlling his/her stress and to identify the intervention methods which effectively target these factors.

iii. Lazarus and Folkman's interpretation of stress focuses on the transaction between people and their external environment (known as the Transactional Model). The model contends that stress may not be a stressor if the person does not perceive the stressor as a threat but rather perceives it as positive or even challenging. And also, if the person possesses or can use adequate coping skills, then stress may not actually be a result because of the stressor. The model proposes that people can be taught to manage their stress and cope with their stressors. They may learn to change their perspective of the stressor and provide them with the ability and confidence to improve their lives and handle all types of stressors.

1.10.2.2 HEALTH REALIZATION/INNATE HEALTH MODEL

The health realization/innate health model of stress is also founded on the idea that stress does not necessarily follow the presence of a potential stressor. Instead of focusing on the individual's appraisal of so-called stressors in relation to his or her own coping skills (as the transactional model does), the health realization model focuses on the nature of thought, stating that it is ultimately a person's thought processes that determine the response to potentially stressful external circumstances. In this model, stress results from appraising oneself and one's circumstances through a mental filter of insecurity and negativity, whereas a feeling of well-being results from approaching the world with a "quiet mind," "inner wisdom," and "common sense".

This model proposes that helping stressed individuals understand the nature of thought -especially providing them with the ability to recognize when they are in the grip of insecure thinking, disengage from it and access natural positive feelings- will reduce their stress.

All human beings suffer from stress. Like happiness or grief, it can't be avoided. In response to daily stresses, human bodies have physical reactions like increased blood pressure, changes in heart rate, respiration, and metabolism. Since everyone is different, the real key is determining your personal tolerance level for stressful situations.

If one can manage stress, instead of letting stress manage the person, a balanced life is possible. Here are some suggestions for managing stress in everyday life:

Dispel the myths of stress. Stress is everywhere, so there is nothing one can do about it. One can arrange his life so that stress does not overwhelm. Managing stress through effective planning, prioritizing and various coping methods should be our goal.

If a person is dealing with a large problem, then break it down into smaller parts. If you have major house cleaning to accomplish, pick out one job and concentrate on getting it done. Once that task is complete, pick out another and so on. There's an old quip: How do you eat an elephant....one bite at a time!

Shed image of perfection. There is a need to do everything perfectly and quickly to build stress. Superman and Superwoman live in comic books, meaning they don't exist in real life.

Stress is a feeling of emotional or physical tension. It can come from any event or thought that makes you feel frustrated, angry, or nervous. Stress is your body's reaction to a challenge or demand. In short bursts, stress can be positive, such as when it helps you avoid danger or meet a deadline. But when stress lasts for a long time, it may harm your health. When stress starts interfering with your ability to live a

34

normal life for an extended period, it becomes even more dangerous. The longer the stress lasts, the worse it is for both your mind and body. You might feel fatigued, unable to concentrate or irritable for no good reason, for example. But chronic stress causes wear and tear on your body, too.

Visualize the stressful situation and think how you can handle it better. Many people feel these "rehearsals" boost self-confidence and give them a positive approach to the task at hand. Meditation or quiet time may help. Ten to twenty minutes of quiet reflection can restore calm and put your troubles in the proper perspectives.

Set a realistic time schedule. Anyone can set a schedule, but the key word is "realistic". Interruptions happen, car batteries die and the phone rings six times when it usually only rings twice. Much as we might like it, life cannot be timed down to the minute. Leave space in the schedule for the unexpected.

Others won't always measure up to our expectations. Don't be disappointed or frustrated when this happens or spend time trying to change the individual. We all have our virtues and shortcomings, so be flexible. Remember the tree that bends in the wind lasts longer than the unyielding tree which breaks.

Strive for balance in your life. A balanced life consists of relaxation time, hobbies, exercise, family time and work time. If others find time for all these things, you can too!

REFERENCES

- Amsa P. (2014) - Human Resource Development in Indian Public Sector Banks - Indian Banking – Managing Transformation, Vol.1, ICFAI University Press, Hyderabad.

- Anas Khan (2015) - An empirical analysis of HR policies on the performance of employees in banking industry: A case study of State Bank of India - International Journal of Multidisciplinary Research and Development, Vol. 2(2).

- Awan K. (2012) - A comparative analysis differences in overall job stress level of permanent employees in private and public sector banks - International Journal of Economics and Management Science, 1 (10).

- Baladev R. Sharma (2011) - A study of Human Resource Management in Indian Banking Industry - Excel Journal of Engineering Technology and Management Science, Vol. I, No. 4.

- Banerjee, Amalesh and Singh, Shrawan Kumar (2001) - Banking and Financial Sector Reforms in India - Deep and Deep Publications Pvt. Ltd., New Delhi.

- Baye M. R. & Jansen D.W. (2006) - Money Banking &Financial Marketing - A.I.T.B.S, Publisher.

- Beehr Tale & Newman M. (1978*). Learning from resilient people: Lessons we can apply to counseling and psychotherapy.* Thousand Oaks, CA: SAGE Publications.

- Bhat M. A. (2013) - Occupational Stress among Bank Employees - An Empirical Study - International Journal of Scientific Research, Vol. 2 (1).

- Canon, M. L. (1935). Foundations of physical education. New Delhi: Metropolitan Book Co. Private Ltd.

- Chitra and V. Mahalakshmi (2015) -A Study on Stress Management among the Employees of Banks - International Journal of Social Science & Interdisciplinary Research, Vol. 4 (1).

- Cooper K & Marshal John. (1978). Workplace stress and indicators of coronary-disease risk. *Academy of Management Journal,* Vol. *31*(3), pp: 686-698.

- Cooper K., Dutton, J., Sonenshein, S., & Grant, A. (1986). A socially embedded model of thriving at work. *Organization Science Vol. 16*(5), pp: 537-549.

- Cox, E. & Smith, E. (1985). Job stress, stress related to performance - based accredited, locus of control, age and gender as related to job stress and satisfaction in teachers and principals. *British Educational Research Journal*, Vol. 16(6), pp: 25-28.

- Deepak Chawala & Neena Sondhi (2014) – Research Methodology – Vikas Publishing House Pvt. Ltd., New Delhi.

- Deolalkar, G.H. (2000) -The Indian Banking Sector: On the Road to Progress – APH Publications, New Delhi.

- E Gordon & K. Natrajan - Banking Theory Law and Practice - Indian financial System & Commercial Banking by Khan Masood Ahmed.

- Enekwe Chinedu Innocent and Agu Charles Ikechukwu (2014) -Stress Management Techniques in Banking Sectors in Nigeria - IOSR Journal of Business and Management, Volume 16, Issue 7.

- Essien Blessing Stephen (2014) - Occupational Stress and Coping Strategies among Female Employees of Commercial Banks in Nigeria - International Journal of scientific research and management, Volume 2, Issue 9.

- Folkman, S & Lazarus, R. (1980). Transforming stress in complex work environments: Exploring the capabilities of middle managers in the public sector. *International Journal of Workplace Health Management, Vol. 6*(1), pp: 66–88.

- Forshaw Shen & Cooper, C. L. (2002) Managers, hierarchies and attitudes: a study of UK managers. *Journal of Managerial Psychology Vol. 19*(1), pp: 41-68.

- G. Gopika (2014) - A Quantitative Analysis on the Correlation between Industrial Experience and Stress Level Changes in Banking Industry - International Journal of Advance Research In Science and Engineering, Vol. No.3, Issue No.12.

- Jones Lee, R. T., & Bright, B. E. (2001). A meta-analytic examination of the correlates of the three dimensions of job burnout. *Journal of Applied Psychology*, Vol. 81: 123-133.

- Lazarus, R. & Folkman, S. (1966). Stress appraisal and coping. New York: Springer.

- Luthans Jackson, Michael P. Leiter, Wilmar B. Schaufeli, & Richard L. Schwab (1988) Maslach Burnout Inventory (MBI): The leading measure of burnout.

- Mahalakshmi and P. Jeyasri. (2015) - A Study on Stress Management Among the Bank Employees in Tirunelveli Distirct at Tamilnadu - International Journal in Management and Social Science, Vol.03, Issue-05.

- Mc Grawth, S. (1970). Comparative study of occupational stress among teachers of private and govt. schools in relation to their age, gender and teaching experience. *International Journal of Educational Planning & Administration*, Vol. 1(2), pp: 151-160.

- McGrath K ,& Vogus, T. (1970). Organizing for resilience. In K. S. Cameron, J. E. Dutton, & R. E. Quinn (Eds.). *Positive Organizational Scholarship: Foundations of a New Discipline* (pp. 94-110). San Francisco: Berrett-Koehler. mindgarden.com. Retrieved May 25, 2012, from http://www.mindgarden.com/products/mbi.htm accessed on 12/12/12.

- Moorhead and Griffin. (1998). Personal environment fit theory and organization: Commensurate dimensions, time perspective and mechanisms. *Journal of Vocational Behaviour*, Vol. 32, pp: 248 267.

- Muniraja Sekhar and B. Sudhir (2014) - HR Management in Commercial Banks in India - Global Journal For Research Analysis.

- Newman Levi L (1979). Guidance to work related stress spice of life or kiss of death? Luxembourg: European commission Retrieved March 5, 2013, from http://www.europa.eu. Int/Comm/employment –social/health – safety/publication/stress-en. Pdf.

- Newman M & Stoltz, P. (1979). *The Adversity Response Profile.* California: Peak Learning.

- NIOSH. (1999). Stress and the police officer (2 ed.). Springfield, IL: Thomas Publishers.

- Prateek Raj, K., Raju, M., Saldanha, D., Chaudhury, S., Basannar, D., Pawar, A., Ryali, V., & Kundeyawala, S. (1983). Psychological well-being of medical students. *Medical Journal Armed Forces of India, Vol. 63*(2), pp: 137-140.

- Selye, J. (1976). Job stressors and their effects on physical health, emotional health and job satisfaction in a university. *Journal of Educational Administration*, Vol. 1, pp: 59-79.

- Sharit, A. & Salvendy, E. (1982). Burnout in Greek teachers: main findings and validity of the Maslach Burnout Inventory. *Work & Stress*, Vol. 11, pp: 94-100.

- Xavior Selvakumar & S. Lawrence Immanuel (2015) - Employees Stress Management in Public and Private Sector Banks in Nagapattinam District-An Analysis - Asia Pacific Journal of Research Vol. I. Issue XXVI.

CHAPTER-II

PROFILE OF SELECTED BANKS

A bank is a financial institution that provides banking and other financial services to its customers. A bank is generally understood as an institution which provides fundamental banking services such as accepting deposits and providing loans. Thus the present chapter is entitled to illustrate a brief overview of the Indian banking sector and also will enlist a detailed profile of selected public and private sector banks of India. This chapter had also outlined certain specified features of job stress-related issues in selected banks under study.

2.1 INTRODUCTION OF BANKING SECTOR

In India, banks are the most important source to finance commercial activities as resources. They act as a mediator between the surplus of funds and deficit of funds and play an important role to boost up the Indian economy by providing financial resources in an appropriate manner. Banking sector contributes 7.7% in Indian GDP and it is considered as the lifeline of the modern economy.

In the words of *Stephenson & Britain* (2011) *"Banks are the custodians and distributors of liquid capital, which is the life-blood of our commercial and industrial activities and upon the prudence of their administration depends the economic well-being of the nation"*. Banks as financial intermediaries channel funds from those who have excess money for investing at interest to those who want to borrow at interest, creating a *'lender-borrower'* relationship. They also provide financial services that reduce the cost of moving funds between borrowers and lenders, leading to a more efficient allocation of resources and faster economic growth. Thus, banks are an essential component of modern economies, not only in terms of turnover but also as primary financiers. Banks provide financial services for the establishment and development of business organizations and that makes banks as a primary tool for providing finance for Women Entrepreneurs.

In India, Banking is one of the oldest systems which was initiated in the 18th century. The main objectives to establish the banking system in India is to provide finance and maintain price stability, to reduce social gaps, to support the financial system, to monitor and support economic policy. The banking sector is the tool to fulfill objectives of monetary policy which regulates money flow in the Indian economy. The banking sector in India is fairly strong and transparent in terms of quality assets and capital adequacy compared to other countries. Presently, Banks are expanding in terms of branches in rural as well as urban areas to promote financial inclusion and to provide a variety of financial products and services suitable for every group of individuals. Recently RBI and Government of India launched various schemes to motivate people to open basic savings bank account like Prime Minister Jan Dhan Yojna (PMDJY), Sukanya Smriddhi Yojna in 2014-15, and Atal Pension Yojna (APY). To enhance the accessibility of credit facilities, government and RBI has initiated various government-sponsored credit programmes, priority sector lending and lead bank schemes through banks.

A bank is an institution which provides banking and financial services by accepting deposits and providing loans to its customers. Nowadays banks have become an integral part of our day to day life by accessing even to a common man and their routines to fulfill the responsibilities and needs related to agriculture, industry and the service sector for the growth and development of all the sections of the society *(Aggarwal, Om Prakash, 2006)*. In totality, banks help and result in the overall growth of the nation in respect of social, economic and structural parameter of development and it inculcates the prosperity, integrity, and opportunity for growth.

Banks play a crucial role in the economic system in terms of maximizing the production and accelerating consumption process and helps in the circulation and exchange of money process. Due to mainly dealing in money it boosts the economic growth by the circulation of it and provides various supports in the economic parameters. With the giant contribution towards an individual and a nation as a whole in the perceptive of development of the economy in a wide context, it increases the capability and boosts the morale which governs the rate of development of the country. The efficiency of the banking sector as a business enterprise can be determined in terms of profitability and output it carries with assets. The principal objective of the banking sector in India is to accelerate and support the stability of finance and economy in the country with the main aspect of gaining profit like other commercial enterprises. Indian Banking Sector has proper planning and guidelines and is concerned with the allocation of resources, sophisticated distribution of income, responsibility towards regional and economic growth, decrease and exclusion of monopoly in terms of trade and industries.

The Indian banking system is mainly categorized into three parts i.e.,

1. RBI (Reserve Bank of India) known as the central bank,

2. Commercial banks and

3. The Co-operative banks.

The Indian banking system can be further classified into scheduled and non-scheduled banks. The reserve bank of India (RBI) is the only right authority and supremacy to control the supply of money and other banking systems within the country. The RBI reserves the cash for the further usage of the banks and in recession time these reserves help the nation and hence it is termed as "Reserve Bank". Systematically, the banking reforms first came into existence for commercial banks so that the financial performance and the operational environment work gala with flexibility and functional autonomy of banks to enhance efficiency, productivity, and profitability.

2.2 HISTORICAL OVERVIEW OF INDIAN BANKING SECTOR

In India, banking started in the 18th Century and the first Bank was established in 1770 as the Bank of Hindustan. During this time banking activity was oriented towards traders only. SBI bank was established in 1955 and in 1969, 14 major banks were nationalized and in 1980, 6 more banks were nationalized to make a strong banking sector in the economy. A lot of reforms have taken place in the Indian banking sector. These can be categorized as before Independence (Before 1947), Second Phase (1947-1991) and Third Phase (After 1991). Before Independence, the first bank of India, Bank of Hindustan was established in 1772 in Calcutta. In this period, various other banks like Allahabad Bank, Punjab National Bank, Central Bank of India were also established but most of them were small in size and there was a high rate of failures. In the second phase, reforms changed the banking industry as 14 banks were nationalized in 1969. NABARD, Regional Rural Banks, EXIM Bank, National Housing Bank, etc. were also established during this phase. Remarkable growth and development in banks started in 1991 when reforms took place after the Narsimhan Committee recommendations. The license was given to private sector entities to give banking services in India. Presently, the Indian banking system is considered a very strong system in developing economies. Currently, 21 Public sector Banks are present in India.

India has two types of banks: Scheduled Banks and Non-scheduled Banks. Scheduled banks are those banks which are included in 2nd schedule of RBI, Act 1935 and Non- Scheduled Banks are those banks which are not included in 2nd Schedule of RBI, Act 1935. Scheduled banks include scheduled commercial banks and scheduled cooperative Banks. Scheduled commercial banks include Public Sector Banks, Private Sector Banks, Foreign Banks, Regional Rural Banks, and Scheduled cooperative banks include Scheduled State Cooperative Banks and Scheduled Urban Cooperative Banks. Presently, in India, there are 21 private sector Banks, 3 local area Banks, 10 small finance Banks, 7 payment Banks, 21 public sector Banks, 4 Financial Institutions, 56 regional rural Banks, and 45 foreign Banks.

Commercial banks are those banks which accept deposit from the public to lend money to borrowers. Private sector banks are those banks where the majority of shares are held by private shareholders. Private sector banks are further divided into two groups -Old private sector banks and New private sector banks, on the basis before nationalization of banks and after the nationalization of banks. Presently there are 22 old private sector banks and 8 new private sector banks in India. Local area banks were established to cover 2 or 3 districts and to provide banking services in the rural area. To serve banking services to the unserved, small finance and payment banks were established on the suggestions of Nachiket Mor Committee. Small finance banks (100 crore capital) were established to achieve financial inclusion and to supply credit to small, micro units, farmers and unorganized sectors. 75% of the credit goes to priority sector lending. Payment Banks only accept a deposit of 1lakh per customer but it cannot lend credit. Public sector banks are the banks where more than 50% of shares are held by the government and shares are listed on the stock exchange. After the suggestions of Narsimhan committee, regional rural banks were established with three sponsors that are a central bank(50%), State Government(15%), Sponsor Banks(35%).

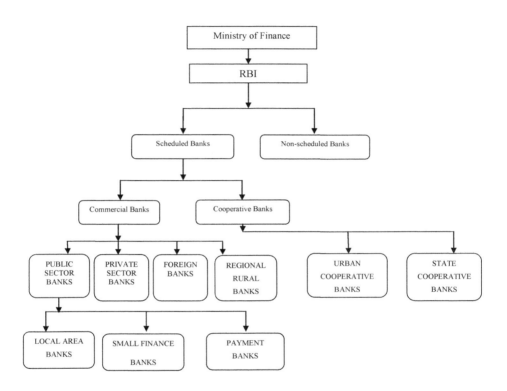

Figure 2.1 Structure of Indian Banking System*

***Source:** Researchers understanding based on published secondary data*

RBI is the prime authority that regulates the entire banking industry. Since the nationalization of banks, all commercial and cooperative banks are growing in terms of size, the volume of transactions and scope of the serving areas, products & services. Banks provide various products and services and we can classify them in three divisions:

(1) Retail Banking;

(2) Trade Finance; and

(3) Treasury Operations.

Retail banking is concerned with individual customers. It facilitates various services like deposits, lending, remittances, bookkeeping, issuing credit card and debit card, cash credit, and overdraft to individual customers. Trade finance is related to business and provides letter of credit, bills of exchange, bill of lading, etc. to business persons. The treasury department of a bank is responsible for balancing and managing the daily cash flow and liquidity of funds within the bank. The department also handles the bank's investments in securities, foreign exchange, asset/liability management, and cash instruments. Common products of banks are debit cards, credit cards, ATM, net banking, cheque, telephone banking, mobile banking, and electronic fund transfer. Nowadays, the banking sector is trying to expand banking services all over India and the main objective behind this is to reach the poor people so that they can also take the benefit of banking services, various government schemes and make speedy payments. Due to the Rupay card given under Pradhan Mantri Jan Dhan Yojna, the use of debit cards has increased tremendously.

2.2.1 RESERVE BANK OF INDIA AND BANKING

The origins of the Reserve Bank of India can be traced to 1926 when the *Royal Commission on Indian Currency and Finance* – also known as the *Hilton-Young Commission* – recommended the creation of a central bank for India to separate the control of currency and credit from the Government and to augment banking facilities throughout the country. The Reserve Bank of India Act of 1934 established the Reserve Bank and set in motion a series of actions culminating in the start of operations in 1935. Since then, the Reserve Bank's role and functions have undergone numerous changes, as the nature of the Indian economy and financial sector changed.

2.2.1.1 HISTORICAL ORIGINS OF THE RESERVE BANK OF INDIA

- **1926:** The Royal Commission on Indian Currency and Finance recommended the creation of a central bank for India.

- **1927:** A bill to give effect to the above recommendation was introduced in the Legislative Assembly, but was later withdrawn due to lack of agreement among various sections of people.

- **1933:** The White Paper on Indian Constitutional Reforms recommended the creation of a Reserve Bank. A fresh bill was introduced in the Legislative Assembly.

- **1934:** The Bill was passed and received the Governor General's assent.

- **1935:** The Reserve Bank commenced operations as India's central bank on April 1 as a private shareholders' bank with a paid up capital of rupees five crores (rupees fifty million).

- **1942:** The Reserve Bank ceased to be the currency issuing authority of Burma (now Myanmar).

- **1947:** The Reserve Bank stopped acting as banker to the Government of Burma.

- **1948:** The Reserve Bank stopped rendering central banking services to Pakistan.

- **1949:** The Government of India nationalized the Reserve Bank under the Reserve Bank (Transfer of Public Ownership) Act, 1948.

- *Starting as a private shareholders' bank, the Reserve Bank was nationalized in 1949. It then assumed the responsibility to meet the aspirations of a newly independent country and its people. The Reserve Bank's nationalization aimed at achieving coordination between the policies of the government and those of the central bank.*

2.2.1.2 FUNCTIONS OF RBI

The functions of the Reserve Bank today can be categorized as follows:

- Monetary policy

- Regulation and supervision of the banking and non-banking financial institutions, including credit information companies

- Regulation of money, forex and government securities markets as also certain financial derivatives

- Debt and cash management for Central and State Governments

- Management of foreign exchange reserves

- Foreign exchange management—current and capital account management

- Banker to banks

- Banker to the Central and State Governments

- Oversight of the payment and settlement systems

- Currency management

- Developmental role

- Research and statistics

Few functions are illustrated in brief:

Monetary Policy of the Country

- The RBI has been tasked to have a monetary policy framework to meet the challenges of the economy and to maintain price stability while keeping in mind the objective of growth.

Inflation control

- The RBI has targeted to keep the mid-term inflation at 4 four percent (+/- 2 percent).

Decides benchmark interest rate

- A six-member Monetary Policy Committee, headed by RBI Governor, decides the benchmark repo rate.

Government's banker

- RBI acts as a banker for both the central as well as state governments.

- It sells and purchases government securities on their behalf.

Regulator of Foreign Exchange

- Foreign Exchange Management Act ("FEMA") envisages that RBI will have a key role in the management of foreign exchange.

- The central bank plays a key role in creating financial awareness among the masses.

- It also supervises if the banks and other financial institutions are doing the job assigned to them regarding financial inclusion.

RBI's Role to Manage Inflation

- Post-2016, RBI has been mandated to manage inflation and growth in their order of priority.

- RBI was constitutionally mandated in 2016 to bring inflation around 4% with a leeway of 2 % on both sides.

- They have successfully brought down the menace of inflation.

- RBI has maintained tighter liquidity and higher real interest rates to control inflation.

2.2.1.3 ORGANISATIONAL FRAMEWORK OF RBI

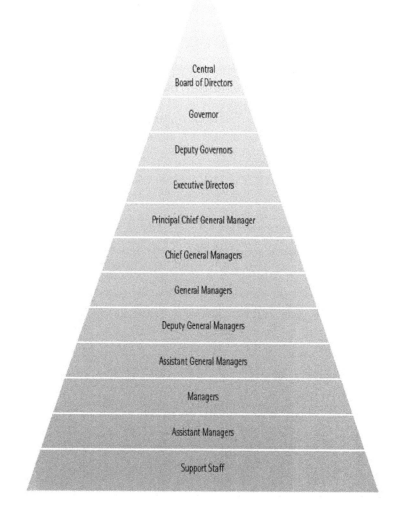

Figure 2.2 Organisational framework of RBI*

***Source:** rbi.co.in (retrieved on 20/10/2018)*

2.2.2 INDIAN SCHEDULED BANKS

Scheduled Banks in India constitute those banks which have been included in the second schedule of RBI Act, 1934. RBI, in turn, includes only those banks in this schedule which satisfy the criteria laid down vide section 42(6) (a) of the Act. Banks which are not included in this schedule are called Non-Scheduled Banks. The Scheduled banks comprise Scheduled Commercial Banks and Scheduled Co-operative Banks.

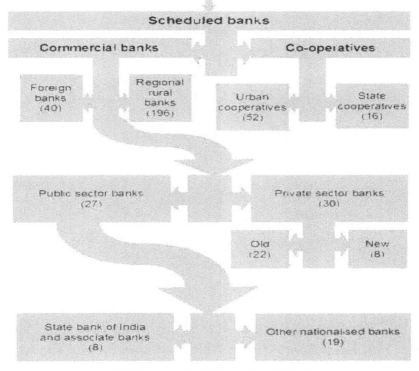

FIG. 2.3 INDIAN BANKING SYSTEM*

*Source-www.rbi.org (assessed on 19th Oct 2018)

Scheduled Commercial banks in India are categorized into different groups according to their ownership and/or nature of the operation. These bank groups are:

1) Public Sector Banks

   • State Bank of India and its associates, and

   • Other Nationalised banks,

2) Private Sector Banks,

3) Foreign Banks, and

4) Regional Rural Banks.

Scheduled Co-operative banks are categorized as:

1) State Co-operative Banks, and

2) Urban Co-operative Banks.

TABLE NO: 2.1 SCHEDULED COMMERCIAL BANKS IN INDIA

Public Sector banks (27)	Private Sector banks (30)	Foreign banks in India (40)	Regional Rural Banks (196)
Nationalized Banks (19)	Old Private Banks (22)	No Category	No Category
SBI & its associates(8)	New Private banks (8)		

Source: Statistical tables relating to banks in India, 2015-16, Reserve Bank of India, Mumbai

2.2.2.1 PUBLIC SECTOR BANKS

Public sector banks are those banks which are owned by the Government. In India, 14 banks were nationalized in 1969 & in 1980, another 6 banks were nationalized. Therefore, in 1980 the number of nationalized banks was 20. At present, there are total 27 Public sector banks in India. Of these 19 are nationalized banks and remaining 8 belong to SBI & its associate banks.

2.2.2.2 PRIVATE SECTOR BANKS

Private sector banks are those banks in which greater parts of stake or equity are held by the private shareholders and not by the government. These banks are the major players in the banking sector as well as in the expansion of business activities in India. The present private sector banks, equipped with all kinds of contemporary innovations, monetary tools, and techniques to handle the complexities are a result of the evolutionary process over two centuries.

There are two categories of private sector banks – "Old" and "New". The old private sector banks have been operating since long and may be referred to as those banks, which are in operation before 1991 and all those banks that have commenced their business after 1991 are called as new private sector banks. Due to economic liberalization and consequent upon greater competition, new private sector entered into the Indian banking.

2.2.2.3 FOREIGN BANKS

In 2005, the Reserve Bank released the "Roadmap for the presence of foreign banks in India" laying out a two-track and gradualist approach aimed at increasing the efficiency and stability of the banking sector in India. One track was the consolidation of the domestic banking system, both in the public and private sector, and the second track was the gradual enhancement of foreign banks in a synchronized manner. The road map was divided into two phases – the first phase spanning the period March 2005 – March 2009 and the second phase beginning after a review of the experience gained in the first phase. However, when the time came to review the experience gained in the first phase, global financial markets were in turmoil and there were uncertainties surrounding the financial strength of banks around the world. At that time, it was considered advisable to continue with the current policy and procedures governing the presence of foreign banks in India.

2.2.2.4 REGIONAL RURAL BANKS

The government of India set up Regional Rural Banks (RRBs) on October 2, 1975. These banks provide credit to the weaker sections of the rural areas, particularly the small and marginal farmers, agricultural laborers, and small entrepreneurs. Initially, five RRBs were set up on October 2, 1975. These banks were created with a view to serve primarily the rural areas of India with basic banking and financial services. The area of operation of RRBs is limited to the area as notified by Government of India covering one or more districts in the state. There are several concessions enjoyed by the RRBs from Reserve Bank of India such as lower interest rates and refinancing facilities from NABARD like lower cash ratio, lower statutory liquidity ratio, lower rate of interest on loans taken from sponsoring banks, managerial and staff assistance from the sponsoring bank and reimbursement of the expenses on staff training. The RRBs are under the control of NABARD. NABARD has the responsibility of laying down the policies for the RRBs, to oversee their operations, provide refinance facilities, to monitor their performance and to attend their problems.

2.2.2.5 CO-OPERATIVE BANKS

A cooperative bank is an institution which is owned by its members. They are the culmination of efforts of people of the same professional or other community which have common and shared interests, problems and aspirations. They cater to services like loans, banking, deposits, etc. like commercial banks but widely differ in their values and governance structures. Cooperative banking includes retail banking carried out by credit unions, mutual savings banks, building societies, and cooperatives, as well as commercial banking services provided by mutual organizations (such as cooperative federations) to cooperative businesses. They are usually democratic set-ups where the board of members is democratically elected with each member entitled to one vote each. In India, they are supervised and controlled by the official banking authorities and thus, have to abide by the banking regulations prevalent in the country.

The cooperative structure in India can broadly be divided into two segments. While the urban areas are served by Urban Cooperative Banks (UCBs), Rural Cooperatives operate in the rural parts of the country. As at end-March 2016, India's co-operative banking sector comprised of 1,574 Urban Cooperative Banks (UCBs) and 93,193 Rural Co-operative Credit Institutions, including short-term and long-term credit institutions.

2.3 CRITERIA FOR SELECTION OF BANKS FOR CURRENT RESEARCH STUDY

The main purpose of this study is to comparatively access the job stress among private and public sector bank employees. Thus, for this purpose selection of banks for research study holds immense importance and it was done on the basis of criterions as illustrated below:

a) Number of employees working in the selected bank.

b) Financial performance of the bank.

c) Availability and number of branches of the bank.

d) Accessibility and feasibility of the research.

The researcher had selected the top 2 public sector banks and 2 private sector banks listed on Indian stock exchanges to balance the study. Among all, State Bank of India and Union Bank of India were selected from public sector banks as they are leading public sector banks. The reason for selection of SBI was that it's the first bank to enter in the Indian banking sector and has the highest financial performance in terms of credit, advances, number of branches, and it also provides varied schemes for women entrepreneurs. In nutshell, it is considered a benchmark in public sector banks. Except for SBI, the other selected bank namely Union Bank of India was selected randomly.

Among private sector banks, ICICI Bank and HDFC Bank are selected as they are leading private sector banks. ICICI Bank and HDFC bank started banking operations from the ignition of private players in the banking sector in India. Both of the selected private sector banks have demonstrated superior performance in terms of business operations and have also provided a sufficient number of employees who were analyzed for job stress variable in the current study.

Thus, the selected banks under study are:

Public Sector Banks under study:

i.   State Bank of India

ii. Union Bank of India.

Private Sector Banks under study:

  i. ICICI Bank Ltd.

  ii. HDFC Bank Ltd.

2.4 PROFILE OF SELECTED BANKS UNDER STUDY

2.4.1 PUBLIC SECTOR BANKS

2.4.1.1 STATE BANK OF INDIA (SBI)

State Bank of India (SBI) is an Indian Public Sector bank. It is a government-owned corporation with its headquarters in Mumbai, Maharashtra. As in December 2013, it had assets of 38800 crores and 17,000 branches, including 190 foreign offices, making it the largest banking and financial services company in India by the value of assets.

The roots of the State Bank of India lie in the first decade of the 19th century when the Bank of Calcutta later renamed the Bank of Bengal, was established on 2 June 1806. The Bank of Bengal was one of three Presidency banks, the other two being the Bank of Bombay (incorporated on 15 April 1840) and the Bank of Madras (incorporated on 1 July 1843). These three presidency banks received the exclusive right to issue paper currency. All three Presidency banks were merged to create the Imperial Bank of India. The Imperial Bank of India became State bank of India on 1 July 1955.

In 2008, the Government of India acquired the Reserve Bank of India's stake in SBI so as to remove any conflict of interest because the RBI is the country's banking regulatory authority. In 1959, the government passed the State Bank of India (Subsidiary Banks) Act, which made eight state banks as associates of SBI. A process of consolidation began on 13 August 2008, when the State Bank of Saurashtra merged with SBI. The State Bank of India and all its associate banks are identified by the same blue keyhole logo. Arundhati Bhattacharya became the first woman to be appointed Chairperson of the bank. On 1 April 2017, SBI merged with its five associate banks named State Bank of Bikaner and Jaipur, State Bank of Mysore, State Bank of Patiala, State Bank of Travancore, State Bank of Hyderabad and with the Bhartiya Mahila Bank.

With the opening of 451 new branches, the branch network of SBI reached 16,784, as in March 2016, of which 65% are in rural and semi-urban areas. To provide an additional convenient service channel to high net worth individuals (Individuals who have net assets more than 7 crores) besides the branch, the bank launched a Priority Banking Centre at Bengaluru on 16th November 2015. This offers personalized services through registered mobile number, enabling valued customers to conduct all non-cash transactions during extended business hours from 8 a.m. to 8 p.m. With an aim of improved customer service, better crowd management, reduction in waiting time and overall reduction in the service time (processing time), bank has rolled out Customer Experience Excellence Project (CEEP), which was accelerated during FY16. 2674 branches were rolled out under CEEP during FY16 and the total number of branches under CEEP was 3006 as in March 2016.

In the last five years, the financial performance of State bank of India shows that the Bank's total deposits amounted to Rs. 17,30,722 crores as in March 2016 showing a compound annual growth rate of 68.4% in five years. Advances for the year 2011-12 were Rs. 8, 67,579 crores and reached to Rs. 14, 63,700 crores registering a CAGR of 67.6%. Investments have also grown substantially at a growth rate of 63.2% in the last five years. Total net interest income of State Bank of India has shown a growth of 34.90% from Rs. 49,282 crores in the year 2013-14 to Rs. 55,015 crores in the year 2014-15. In the year 2015-16, net interest income increased at a rate of 3.96%. Net profit showed a fluctuating trend in five years. 2013-14 and 2015-16 was not a good period for SBI in case of net profit.

2.4.1.2 UNION BANK OF INDIA

The bank was originally incorporated in Mumbai as "The Union Bank of India Limited" under the Companies Act 1913, on November 11, 1919. After nationalization, the name of the bank was changed to "Union Bank of India". The Head Office of the bank is situated in Mumbai. The bank is a public sector unit, with 60.85% share capital held by the Government of India and the rest 39.15% of share capital is held by institutions, individuals and others. The Father of the Nation Mahatma Gandhi inaugurated this bank in 1921. The bank's vision should be a shared vision, i.e. the staff at all levels should actively involve in the transformation process. Union Bank of India from the beginning have reached Himalayan heights, now ranked third among the nationalized banks. Its branches are spread all over the country and serving more than 26 million customers. Union Bank of India has come a long way, fostering India's dreams. For over nine decades, the bank has always put the customer before everything else and made them the center of the universe. The bank has the habit of making profits consistently for the last 91 years. On the technology front, the bank has taken early initiatives and 100% of its branches are computerized. Over the years, Union Bank of India has earned the reputation of being a techno-savvy bank and is one of the front runners amongst public sector banks in the field of technology. It is one of the pioneer banks, which launched the Core Banking Solution in 2002. The business of the bank is principally divided into three main areas: Corporate Financial Services, Retail Financial Services, and Agricultural Financial Services. Many innovative products are developed using the technological platform. With its prudent management and good governance, banks non- performing assets were comparatively lower. In the post-reforms period i.e. from 1993 to 1996, the bank doubled itself in size. The first safe deposit vault was formally opened on 22 April 1939. The bank worked with Export Credit Guarantee Corporation of India for encouraging the exporters to insure themselves against buyers default or exchange difficulties in the buyer's country. Union Bank of India was one of the earliest banks to obtain and operate whole turnover export finance guarantee from ECGC. The bank has several strengths such as a strong branch network evenly distributed, an extremely good work culture with a fair standard of customer services and a history of effective execution of projects. Union Bank of India is one in top three nationalized banks in India, with a global presence.

The Union Bank of India is the first bank to implement CBS at RRBs. In this initiative, the bank is providing implementation, training, and hand-holding support to the RRBs. The bank is a pioneer in extending high-tech products to customers at the metro and rural centres.

Union Bank of India is firmly committed to consolidating and maintaining its identity as a leading, innovative commercial bank, with a proactive approach to the changing needs of the society through the number of products and services made available to its valuable customers. Today, with its efficient, value-added services, sustained growth, consistent profitability and development of new technologies, UBI has ensured complete customer delight, living up to its image of, "GOOD PEOPLE TO BANK WITH". The key to the success of any organization lies with its people.

VISION Statement of UBI:

"To become the bank of the first choice in our chosen areas by building beneficial and lasting relationships with customers through a process of continuous improvement".

At Union Bank of India they have the vision to be:

- The largest nationalized bank in India, with a global presence.

- A financial supermarket, with leadership in identified spaces.

- A top shareholder wealth creator where growth is a passion.

- A young, innovative and adaptive organization leveraging its experienced workforce.

- A bank where customers are supreme and the brand admired by all stakeholders.

- An organization that cares for society and demonstrates the best corporate governance.

The following strategies were identified by the bank for achieving the vision:

a) Grow faster -- 5% over the growth rate of peer banks in business.

b) Do things differently -new methods of doing business.

c) Everyone to contribute— share the vision and take effort to realize it.

d) Challenge the mindset— proves themselves that they can change.

MISSION Statement of UBI:

- To be a customer-centric organization known for its differentiated customer service.

- To offer a comprehensive range of products to meet all the financial needs of customers.

- To be a top creator of shareholder wealth through a focus on profitable growth.

- To be a young organization leveraging on technology and an experienced workforce.

- To be the most trusted brand, admired by all stakeholders.

- To be a leader in the area of Financial Inclusion.

Principles of Bank Management:

- Transparency: Decision making in all areas is conducted in a transparent manner. The management at UBI is open, consistent and system driven.

- Open door: Management is accessible at all times to people and receptive to ideas and grievances.

- Teamwork and cohesiveness: Collective decision making and shared responsibility are the need of the hour.

- Loyalty to the institution: Management's loyalty should be solely with the institution. They do not desire or demand any personal loyalty.

Business Objectives of UBI:

- **Customer Service:** From customer satisfaction to customer delight. Customer satisfaction can be achieved through constant effort to bring the products and services. Customer delight is completely the initiative of the individual employee of UBI. In today's market place, customer retention is the most crucial task.

- **Profits:** It is the quality and not the size of the balance sheet. Identify profit centres and give them preferred attention in terms of infrastructure, skills, technology and decision making.

- **Technology:** Technology is the driving force of today's banking products like anywhere banking, anytime banking, and funds transfer are to be taken care of.

- **Re-Setting Manpower**: Extended hours of counter- service, relationship management, etc. will enable the customer to realize the untapped productivity of the bank.

- **Business Strategies**: Low-cost deposits: Bank's portfolio of low-cost deposits, i.e. savings and current deposits by identifying ways to improve services to customers.

- **Fee-Based Services**: Fee-based services will bring more income to the bank. They are to be marked effectively and focused attention on rendering dependable and timely services.

- **Counter Service Efficiency**: Counter service options like single window, tellers, express DD counters and Tele-banking.

Awards and Commendations of UBI:

Union Bank of India is the proud recipient of many awards and recognition for its services.

a. On 28th October 2010 the Dale Carnegie Leadership award for the bank's transformation initiatives undertaken through project Nav Nirman from Dale Carnegie Training.

b. In 2010 Association of Business Communicators of India (ABCI) Gold award for marketing and brand communications. This award is in recognition of the transformation process undertaken by the bank from ABCI.

c. The prestigious Banking Technology awards 2009 for best use of business intelligence from IBA-IFCI.

d. The prestigious Skoch-Challenger award 2009 for excellence in capacity building through the innovative concept of 'Village Knowledge Centre' as part of financial inclusion initiatives.

e. In 2008-09 National awards for excellence in lending to micro-enterprises.

f. In 1972-1973 excellent performance award on the exports front by the Ministry of Commerce, Government of India. That was the first award received by the bank from an outside agency.

g. In 1985 the bank was awarded first prize in region 'B', second prize in region 'C' and fourth prize in region 'A' by the Reserve Bank of India for successfully implementation of the official language policy of the Government in the year 1984.

h. Prestigious Golden Peacock National Training award 1998 for the best training provider in the country by the Institute of directors (2 times).

i. Reserve Bank of India Rajabhasha Shield for the year 1995 to 1996 and 18 offices of the bank were honored for better implementation of official language policy in their respective Regions.

j. Corporate Excellence award for reputation on 26th June 2006 from Rotary International.

k. UBI was ranked as the 275th most valuable Global banking brand for the calendar year 2009, up from 351st rank in 2008. The brand value rating for Union Bank is A+ (A means strong) compared to BB (BB means Average) in the previous year. The ranking is carried by brand value, the bank's brand value increased by 148% during the calendar year 2009.

l. 7th Strongest bank in Asia-Pacific Region in 2009, from the Asian Banker.

m. Special citation at FIIA Awards 2009, Singapore for its 100% achievement through in-house efforts.

n. The Gold Trophy and a Certificate in the Elite class for excellence in marketing and Brand communication by Association of Business Communication of India (ABCI) in March 2015.

TABLE 2.2 ORGANIZATIONAL PROFILE OF UBI

(AS ON DATE 31.3.2017)

Sl.No.	Profile parameters	
1	Establised	1919
2.	Head office	Mumbai
3.	Shareholding pattern:	No. of shares held
	Government of India	28,00,00,000 (55.43%)
	Non- Residents(FIIs / OCBs / NRIs)	8,81,69,325 (17.46%)
	Banks / Financial institutions / Insurance companies	1,98,10,523 (3.92%)
	Mutual Funds / UTI	4,42,74,751 (8.76%)
	Domestic companies / Private corporate bodies/Trusts	2,32,58,361 (4.61%)
	Resident individuals	4,96,04,940 (9.82%)
	Total	50,51,17,900 (100)
4	Number of branches	2805
5	Foreign branches	2
6	Number of ATMs	2500
7	Computerisation/ Core Banking Solution (CBS)	100%
8	Number of staff	27772
9	Subdidiaries / Joint venture	2

Source: UBI Annual Report (2016-17)

Strength / Opportunities of UBI:

The growth for UBI in the coming years is likely to be fueled by the following factors:

- Continued effort to increase low-cost deposit base would ensure improvement in NIMs and hence earnings.

- Increasing retail thrust would lead to higher business growth.

- Strong economic growth would generate higher demand for funds pursuant to higher corporate demand for credit on account of capacity expansion.

- The bank is working on a business process reengineering exercise to optimize CBS gains.

- Greater focus on profitable segments, exclusive cadre for corporate clients.

- Cluster-based approach to developing SME accounts.

Weakness / Threats of UBI

The risks that could ensue to UBI in time to come are as under:

- UBI is currently operating at a low CAR of below 11.5 %. Insufficient capital may restrict the growth prospects of the bank going forward.

- The age profile of the employees is in the range of 47-48 years. Viewed from a certain perspective this could have a negative connotation as, for example when it is compared to the age profile of customers of the banking industry. It has been estimated that 55% of the customer population today come from the age group below 25 years. Today relationship building is very important and hence staff with a higher age profile might experience difficulties in relating to the younger segment.

- Stiff competition, especially in the retail segment, could impact retail growth of UBI and hence slowdown in earnings growth.

- Slow down in the domestic economy would pose concern over credit off-take, thereby impacting earnings growth.

2.4.2 PRIVATE SECTOR BANKS

2.4.2.1 ICICI BANK

ICICI Bank was established by the Industrial Credit and Investment Corporation of India (ICICI), an Indian financial institution, as a wholly owned subsidiary in 1994. The parent company was formed in 1955 as a joint venture of the World Bank, India's public-sector banks and public-sector insurance companies to provide project financing to Indian industry.

The bank was initially known as the 'Industrial Credit and Investment Corporation of India Bank' before it changed its name to the abbreviated ICICI Bank. The parent company was later merged with the bank. It launched internet banking operations in 1998.

Industrial Credit and Investment Corporation of India (ICICI) Bank is an Indian multinational banking and financial services company headquartered in Mumbai, Maharashtra. Since 2014, it is the second largest bank in India in terms of assets and market capitalization.

It offers a wide range of banking products and financial services for corporate and retail customers through a variety of delivery channels and specialized subsidiaries in the areas of investment banking, life, non-life insurance, venture capital, and asset management. The bank currently has a network of 4,867 branches and 14,367 ATMs in India and has a presence in 19 countries including India.

ICICI Bank is one of the Big Four banks of India, along with State Bank of India, Punjab National Bank and Bank of Baroda. The bank has subsidiaries in the United Kingdom, Russia, and Canada; branches in United States, Singapore, Bahrain, Hong Kong, Sri Lanka, Qatar, and Dubai International Finance Centre; and representative offices in United Arab Emirates, China, South Africa, Bangladesh, Thailand, Malaysia, and Indonesia.

ICICI Bank added 297 branches to its network in the year 2016. During the fiscal year 2016, the bank expanded its network to 4,450 branches. The Bank's automation footprint has also multiplied. While expanding the branch network, the bank has focused on enhancing customer convenience through its automation strategy. The Bank is also the first in the country to create a network of fully automated Touch Banking branches, available 24X7.

Bank's total deposits amounted to Rs.4,21,426 crores as in March 2016 showing a growth of 68.7% over the previous five year's. Advances for the year 2011-12 were Rs.2,53,728 crores and reached to Rs. 4,35,264 crores registering a growth of 66.7% in the year 2015-16. Investments have grown by 64.5% in the five years. Total net interest income of ICICI Bank has shown a growth of 60% from Rs. 10,734 crores in the year 2011-12 to Rs. 21,224 crores in the year 2015-16. As far as net NPA is concerned, the amount has increased substantially in five years which is not a good sign for banks. Net profit increased registering a strong growth by 78.3% except in the year 2013-14. Earnings per share have also reached to Rs. 16.75 per share in 2015-16 as against to Rs. 5.61 per share in 2011-12. It shows that the bank is fulfilling its commitment towards shareholders.

2.4.2.2 HDFC BANK

HDFC Bank was incorporated on 30th August 1994. A new private sector bank promoted by Housing Development Finance Corporation Ltd. (HDFC), is a preemie housing finance company. Housing Development Finance Corporation Limited (HDFC) was amongst the first to receive an 'in principle' approval from the Reserve Bank of India (RBI) to set up a bank in the private sector, as part of RBI's liberalization of the Indian Banking Industry in 1994. The bank was incorporated in August 1994 in the name of 'HDFC Bank Limited', with its registered office in Mumbai, India. HDFC Bank commenced operations as a Scheduled Commercial Bank in January 1995.

HDFC Bank is headquartered in Mumbai. As of March 31, 2015, the Bank's distribution network was at 4,014 branches in 2,464 cities. Customers across India are serviced through multiple delivery channels such as Phone Banking, Net Banking, Mobile Banking, and SMS based banking.

The Bank also has a network of 11,766 ATMs across India.

The authorized share capital of the Bank was Rs. 550 crore as on 31st March 2015. The paid-up share capital of the Bank as on the said date was Rs.501, 29,90,634. The HDFC Group holds 21.67 % of the Bank's equity and about 18.87 % of the equity is held by the ADS / GDR Depositories (in respect of the bank's American Depository Shares (ADS) and Global Depository Receipts (GDR) Issues). 32.57 % of the equity is held by Foreign Institutional Investors (FIIs) and the Bank has 4,41,457 shareholders.

Times Bank Limited (another new private sector bank promoted by Bennett, Coleman & Co. / Times Group) was merged with HDFC Bank Ltd., effectively on February 26, 2000. This was the first merger of two private banks in the New Generation Private Sector Banks. Later, the amalgamation of Centurion Bank of Punjab with HDFC Bank was formally approved by Reserve Bank of India, on May 23, 2008, to complete the statutory and regulatory approval process. The amalgamation added significant value to HDFC Bank in terms of increased branch network, geographic reach, and customer base, and a bigger pool of skilled manpower.

HDFC Bank caters to a wide range of banking services covering commercial and investment banking on the wholesale side and transactional / branch banking on the retail side. The bank has three key business segments: wholesale banking, treasury, and retail banking.

Mission:

HDFC Bank's mission is to be a World Class Indian Bank. The objective is to build sound customer franchises across distinct businesses so as to be the preferred provider of banking services for target retail and wholesale customer segments, and to achieve healthy growth in profitability, consistent with the bank's risk appetite. The bank is committed to maintaining the highest level of ethical standards, professional integrity, corporate governance, and regulatory compliance. HDFC Bank's business philosophy is based on five core values: Operational Excellence, Customer Focus, Product Leadership, People and Sustainability.

Technology:

HDFC Bank operates in a highly automated environment in terms of information technology and communication systems. All the bank's branches have online connectivity, which enables the bank to offer speedy funds transfer facilities to its customers. Multi-branch access is also provided to retail customers through the branch network and Automated Teller Machines (ATMs).

The Bank has prioritized its engagement in technology and the internet as one of its key goals and has already made significant progress in web-enabling its core businesses. In each of its businesses, the Bank has succeeded in leveraging its market position, expertise and technology to create a competitive advantage and build market share.

REFERENCES

- Aggarwal, Om Prakash. 2006," Innovations in Banking & Insurance", Himalaya Publishing House, Mumbai.

- Bancassurance – An Introduction. Hand book published by Indian Bankers Association, 2014. Bombay

- Chatley, Pooja. Kaur, Khushdip & Marwaha, Rajesh (2008). Bancassurance: The new wave in the life insurance sector in Uppal, R.K. (Ed), Challenges and Opportunities for Banks in India. New Delhi, Mahamaya Publishing House. 1st edition, Pg. no.185-196.

- CIFP Knowledge Series- Bancassurance: Convergence of Banking and Insurance 2010, pg.no 1-23

- Desai, Vasant (2006) "Banks & Institutional Management" Himalaya Publishing House, Mumbai, Page 152

- Draft Guidelines for diversification into Insurance business by banks/financial institutions, Circular published by Reserve Bank of India, August 3, 2000.

- Gujral. Tripti M., 2014, An Impact of Bancassurance product on Banking business in India – An In-depth study", A PH.D. Thesis submitted to Maharaja Sayajirao University, Baroda

- Karunagaran, A. (2006). Bancassurance: A Feasible Strategy for Banks in India? Reserve Bank of India Occasional Papers, volume 27(3), pg. no.125-162.

- Lang. Levy. "Bancassurance – Convergence of Banking and Insurance, The risk effects of combining Banking, securities and insurance activities." Journal of Economics & Business, Pg no 485-497

- Neelamegam, R, & Veni, K. Pushpa.2009, "Bancassurance - An Emerging Trend in Indian service Sector" Indian Journal of Marketing, pg. no.49-54.

- Ravichandaran, K. 2007,"Recent trends in Insurance Industry in India", Textbook published by Abhijeet Publications, New Delhi

- Report of the committee on Bancassurance, Insurance Regulatory and Development Authority (IRDA), June 7, 2011.

- S. Saveeta, (2005) "Commercial banks in India" Deep and deep publications, New Delhi, Page. 51

- Saghir, Ahmed, Financial reforms in India, Mittal publications, 2006, New Delhi, Page 46

- Saravanan, S., 2014,"Bancassurance channel- A SWOT Analysis", Abhinav National Monthly Referred Journal of Research in Commerce & Management Volume No.2, Issue No.4 ,ISSN 2277-1166

- Sreesha, C.H., 2014, "Bancassurance in India-a case study of SBI ", New York, Lambert Academic Publishing, pg.no. 4-25

- Stephenson M & Britain Steven. (2011). "Bancassurance: The Lessons of Global Experience in Banking and Insurance Collaboration", London, VRL Knowledge Bank Ltd, Paterson's publishing House.

- Vittal, N (2001). The emerging challenges: Strategies and solutions for Indian banking. IBA Bulletin 23(3): pg 9-15.

WEBSITES:

- www.rbi.org.in

- www.sbi.co.in

- www.icicibank.com

- www.hdfc.co.in

- http://www.rediff.com/money/report/sbi-eyes-rs-2-trillion-home-loan-portfolio-by-march-2015/20121019.htm

- http://www.financialexpress.com/news/sbi-equals-hdfc-in-housing-finance/634669

- http://www.rupeetimes.com/news/car_loans/icici_bank_forecasts_ 15_credit_growth_in_201011_3253.html

CHAPTER-III

RESEARCH METHODOLOGY

The blueprint of any research project requires considerable attention to the research methods and the proposed data analysis. Within this section i.e chapter III, the author has attempted to provide some information about the research plan for the current study. This section also elaborates the literature cited for current research which acts as a navigator to reach the aim of the study.

3.1 RESEARCH – AN OVERVIEW

"All progress is born of inquiry. Doubt is often better than over-confidence, for it leads to inquiry, and inquiry leads to invention"

This above statement of Hudson Maxim, a famous US inventor had to say in the context of the importance of research. He is very correct in conveying that increased amount of research makes the progress possible.

Research in common parlance denotes a search for knowledge and it can also be defined as a scientific investigation. If a dictionary is consulted for understanding this term, it is said to be a careful investigation or inquiry specially through search for new facts in any branch of knowledge(Avula, Pandey, & Avula, 2013).

Research is a process where the researcher collects, analyses and interprets information to answer questions. But it qualifies as research only once it has certain characteristics. It must, as far as possible, be controlled, rigorous, systematic, valid and verifiable, empirical and critical.

Thus, in the quest of gaining knowledge and discovering new techniques with regards to the research problems which has been discussed in this research study, a systematic approach has been conducted for the investigation and inquiry of the same. Hereby, this chapter discusses the methodology adopted to execute this study to attain the required objective by ensuring the basic characteristics to be eligible as research work.

The present research problem is to study the "***Job Stress Among Employees of Banking Industry (A Comparative Study of Selected Public and Private Sector Banks in Haryana)***"

- **Background of The Topic**

The present study is conducted to analyze the level of stress experienced by employees working in the banking industry (both public and private). The results of this study will be helpful in understanding the type of factors and job conditions that lead to stress and also the various methods used to cope with stress. The results of the study would also help the policymakers to draw up new policies to manage the problems of job stress in bank employees.

Therefore, the present research on "*Job Stress among Employees of Banking Industry (A Comparative Study of Selected Public and Private Sector Banks in Haryana)*" is based to cover the following Research Methodology.

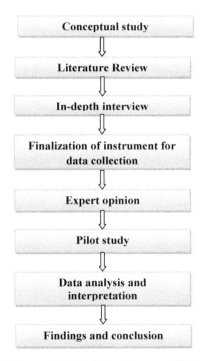

Figure 3.1 Research Methodology Process (Flow Chart)*
*Source: *Researchers own understanding*

3.2 RESEARCH PARADIGM

The chapter focuses on the main hypothetical positions that establish the designs of this study. It requires describing the hypothetical basis that drives the methodology directed towards achieving the aim and objectives of the research.

Many arguments, criticism, and debates are important in the progress of philosophy and therefore it is important to understand both sides of an argument because research problems require eclectic design, which draws from more than one tradition (Adelopo, 2010). In answering the main questions of this study, the research methodology framework, as depicted in the Research Paradigm Onion (Figure 3.2) is used.

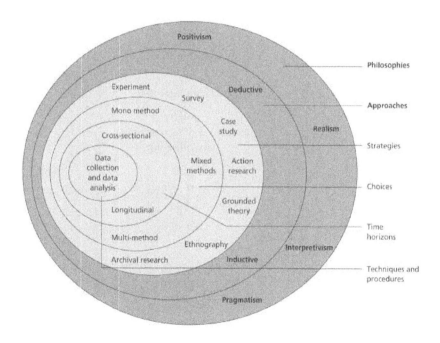

Figure 3.2 Research Paradigm Onion
Source:https://www.researchgate.net/profile/Andrej_Fidersek/publication/283013573 /figure /fig4 /AS:286623037181955@1445347665504/Figure-6-Research-Onion.png

The research paradigm onion is lined above clearly explaining the concept of research methodology Figure 3.2 depicts that the first layer contains the philosophical stances associated with the philosophies. Philosophy is the basic idea of any research that should have been developed at an early stage of research. Since the philosophy execution, a researcher has to fix up the key research approach whether it is deductive or inductive. Once a research approach has been fixed, the researcher has to choose the research style that he will use to collect and analyze data such as Grounded Theory as well as case study, experiment or survey.

Forthcoming in layer 4 as per the above diagram, a researcher has to define how he wishes to use the methods of research in which he will actually design and collect data. Subsequently, a researcher should decide the scope of the study, where he has only two-time horizon choices. These are cross-sectional, which is a short-term study, and longitudinal, which is a research carried out over a longer period of time.

The final layer of the onion moves the research design further into the practicalities of data collection and analysis. This is where a researcher needs to decide that what methods of data collection will work best and what type of analysis he makes use of to frame the results of his research question on the basis of all previous decisions he has made.

The research methodology is a term that basically means the science of how research is done scientifically. It is a way to systematically and logically solve a problem, help us understand the process not just the product of research, and analyzes methods in addition to the information obtained by them. *(Clairewait, July 22, 2010)*. The research methodology framework can be defined as the process which starts from the idea of research and ends with the application and analysis of research methods and techniques for the purpose of the conclusion of the research.

3.3 REVIEW OF LITERATURE

A **literature review** is a body of text that aims to review the critical points of current knowledge including substantive findings as well as theoretical and methodological contributions to a particular topic. Literature reviews are secondary sources, and as such, do not report any new or original experimental work. Also, a literature review can be interpreted as a review of an abstract accomplishment. Most often associated with academic-oriented literature, such as a thesis, a literature review usually precedes a research proposal and results section. Its main goals are to situate the current study within the body of literature and to provide context for the particular reader. The ability to review, and to report on relevant literature is a key academic skill. A literature review:

- Situates your research focus within the context of the wider academic community in your field;

- Reports your critical review of the relevant literature

- Identifies a gap within the literature that our research will attempt to address.

The process of conducting and reporting your literature review can help you clarify your own thoughts about your study. It can also establish a framework within which to present and analyze the findings. After reading your literature review, it should be clear to the reader that you have up-to-date awareness of the relevant work of others, and that the research question you are asking is relevant. However, don't promise too much! Be wary of saying that your research will solve a problem, or that it will change practice. It would be safer and probably more realistic to say that your research will 'address a gap', rather than that it will 'fill a gap'.

In the current research study the review of literature has been sub-divided into following sub-segments based on the variables of study:

3.3.1 Review of Literature related with Job Stress

3.3.2 Review of Literature related with Job Stress in the Banking Sector

3.3.3 Review of Literature related with Consequences of Job Stress

3.3.4 Review of Literature related with Coping methods of Job Stress

3.3.1 REVIEW OF LITERATURE RELATED WITH JOB STRESS

The study carried out by ***Kotteeswari & Sharief in the year 2014*** tried to find out the factors causing job stress and explain how the job stress factors were influencing the performance of the employees working in BPOs. The study made an attempt to find out the modern coping strategies followed by the employer and employee to overcome their stress for the purpose of improving their performance. The results from the study revealed that majority of the employees agree that the job stress factors or job stress are affecting their performance. They are not able to concentrate on their work properly. The study also found that both the employer and the employee are following some stress coping strategies to overcome the stress.

A study by **Manzoor et al. (2011)** evaluated the level of job satisfaction and job stress among the faculty members of the universities in Lahore, Pakistan. The main objective of the study was to identify the determinates of job stress. From the study, it was concluded that employees were mostly satisfied with their jobs and committed to their organizations. The level of satisfaction was dependent on: Satisfaction with the organization's Management. This study revealed that professional approach during the job by employer, peers, and employee himself has a statistically significant impact on the level of job satisfaction. The study revealed that proper facilities at job, salary, bonus, shares, etc lead to a positive impact on the level of job satisfaction.

To investigate the impact job stress has on employees' productivity and commitment, a study by **Ekienabor E. E. (2016)** was conducted in Okada. The purpose of the study was to find out the impact job stress has on the productivity and commitment of employees'. Primary data sources were used for checking the level of stress and its impact. The questionnaire was used as the primary data collection instrument and the qualitative data was determined through observations, articles, and recent research papers. The major findings of the study were that job stress has an impact on the productivity of employees. This in large extent is due to the working environment as employees indicated that they are not too happy with their working environment. In addition, the study also found that there is an impact of job stress on employees' commitment. This is because employees feel uncared for by the organization.

Murali et al. (2017) also analyzed the impact of job stress on employees' performance. The objective of the study was to study and examine the effect of time pressure on employee performance & the effect of workload on employee performance. The chosen research design to examine the impact of stress on employee performance was explanatory or causal research design. The study derived various conclusions from the findings. It was found that time pressure and role ambiguity have a significant adverse influence on employee performance. It is, therefore, seemed that employees undergo job stress when they are pushed-right to the wall and pressurized to complete their task within an unreasonable time provided by their employers' or superiors. Adding on, less support from managers in completing the assignment has led to a high level of job stress and dissatisfaction in job performance. One of the case studies in Malaysia revealed that employees' get extremely stressed-out when they are forced to submit their work on time to their employer without accepting any given reason.

Khuong and Yen (2016) stated in their study about the effects of stress on employee job performance. The purpose of this research was to analyze the effects of five working factors including work overload, role ambiguity & role conflict, working relationship, career development, and working environment on job stress and employee job performance. For the study, the conceptual framework and hypotheses were constructed based on previous theoretical and empirical studies. After analyzing data, model and almost proposed hypothesis were accepted. From the research findings, it was concluded that all working factors had a significant and positive influence on job stress and negative influence on employee job performance. As a result, these working factors are effective tools to explain and predict job stress and employee job performance.

Riaz et al. (2016) investigated the relationship between job stress and employee job satisfaction in the Nursing Sector. The main objective of the study was to investigate the relationship between job stress and employee job satisfaction and to find out the authentic variable of job stress that affects employee job satisfaction. With a descriptive design, the study elaborated the past studies and researches undergone with same variables. If employees feel great stress on their job and employees are less satisfied with their job then the performance of the organization will be affected. Thus, it is important for an organization to understand the needs of its employees and give them the environment which satisfies them and fulfill their needs. The study found that nurses of hospitals are satisfied with their job and experience a little bit of stress on their job. The performance of the hospital depends upon the performance of the nurses and doctors of the hospital. For enhancing the performance of the nurses, the management should provide training to their nurses to control the stress and attain a high level of job satisfaction. The management should also provide a friendly and supportive environment for their nurses. The different reward systems like appraisal, compensation, etc. will be of great help in increasing the level of job satisfaction.

Narban et al. (2016) in their study stated that occupational stress (Job stress/Work stress) relates to one's job. The researchers tried to study the concept of occupational stressors and identify the impacts of occupational stressors. The exploration of occupational-stress/work-stress/job-stress has been relatively a neglected area of research among industrial/organizational psychologists. It is concluded and suggested that empirical research in the domain of occupational stress and employee health should consider and map the impact and influences of these factors viz., 1. environmental, 2. personal, 3. process, 4. human consequences, 5. organizational consequences, 6. role dynamics, 7. time of stress and 8. adaptive responses. Stress is found to be additive and there is also a positive relationship between role stressors and job stress. Occupational stress (Job stress/Work stress) need to be kept harnessed and minimized to provide a conducive work environment in the organization.

Moreover, *Ratnawat & Jha (2014)* also highlighted the impact of occupational stress on employee performance and focused research on the relationship between stress and job performance. A conceptual model was proposed towards the end to study the impact of stress on employee job performance. The research found that for male factory workers the financial problems/low wages followed by poor physical environment, dual career, threat to job security, social/physical isolation, personal/family problem, no role in decision making, boring repetitive work, frustration over career ambition,and harassment and bullying were significant stressors in decreasing order of importance while for female workers the stressors were in terms of dual career, financial problems/low wages, personal/family problems, social/physical isolation, poor physical environment, frustration over career ambition, boring repetitive work, threat to job security, no role in decision making,and harassment and bullying in the decreasing order of intensity.

Awadh et al. (2015) in their research tried to determine workplace stress and its effects on employee performance. The researcher also tried to establish the effects of job demand on employees' performance and determine the effects of time pressure on employees' performance. The research design was a descriptive survey design and the target population research was the 2300 employees of public service department in the seven sub-counties of the County Government of Kilifi. In determining workplace stress and its effects on employees' performance the study revealed that time pressure is one of the main factor that hinders performance due to the fact employees reach a burnout level that they can no longer produce effectively. Furthermore, they lack work-life balance and thus stressed on how to balance the two which hinders their performance in a huge percentage. The physical demand of the job also affects employees performance to a certain level though not as much as time pressure however if the physical demand increases higher it will have a direct impact on the time pressure.

The purpose of the study by *Gharib et al. (2016)* was to determine the levels of job stress among the academic staff at Dhofar University, to measure the job performance level, and determine the impact of the job stress factors (workload, role conflict, and role ambiguity) on job performance. For this purpose, 102 structured questionnaires were collected from the academic staff of Dhofar University, Sultanate of Oman. Obtained results from the research questionnaires were analyzed by using Multiple Regression analysis, to find the impact of job stress on job performance. Results showed that the level of job stress of academic staff was medium and sometimes low. In addition, the level of Job performance was somewhat high. Moreover, it was found that workload had a positive statistical effect on job performance, while role conflict had a negative statistical effect on job performance. Finally, role ambiguity does not significantly affect job performance.

"Job stress and job satisfaction are important factors affecting workforce productivity" as discussed in the research of *Hoboubi et al. (2017)*. The study was carried out to investigate the job stress, job satisfaction, and workforce productivity levels, to examine the effects of job stress and job satisfaction on workforce productivity, and to identify factors associated with productivity decrement among employees of Iranian petrochemical industry. The results of the study showed that the levels of employees' perceived job stress and job satisfaction were moderate-high and moderate, respectively. Also, their productivity was evaluated as moderate. Although the relationship between job stress and productivity indices was not statistically significant, the positive correlation between job satisfaction and productivity indices was statistically significant. Thus, it was concluded that corrective measures are necessary to improve the shift work system and "role insufficiency" and "role ambiguity" should be improved and supervisor support must be increased to reduce job stress and increase job satisfaction and productivity.

3.3.2 REVIEW OF LITERATURE RELATED WITH JOB STRESS IN BANKING SECTOR

A study by *Jayasinghe and Mendis (2017)* was carried out in the Northern region of Sri Lanka, with the primary objective of understanding the effect of stress on bank employees and its impact over performance. Secondly, the research also tried to identify the effect of stress relating to job, organizational and individual factors and their relationships over performance. A correlation test was carried out to determine the relationship between variables. To test the effect of stress on performance, a regression analysis was carried out. The study revealed that the relationship between stress and performance was negative and concluded that the stress was impacting over the performance of the employees of the banking industry.

Masood (2013) in his study tried to evaluate the effect of job stress over employee retention and organization efficiency and to empirically study job stress that directly affects employee retention at different levels of age people. The research also tried to empirically study job stress that directly affects employee retention at different levels of income groups and measure how much job stress plays a function in increasing disappointment among employees. The current study was arranged among employees of the banking sector of Pakistan and as it is employee-based research, the choice has been meticulously made in terms of gender and age. The results revealed that employees are required to work with energy, ability, and determination even if they are not provided with the support; they need to perform their tasks with honesty. They are more focused to avoid stress and it directly affects their performance.

Roslan (2011) carried out a study to determine factors of work stress among the Bank Rakyat's employees. The study aimed to determine whether there were any statistically significant differences in the respondents' level of work stress by demographic factors (gender, status, education qualification, job position and length of service). Results showed that there was no statistically significant difference in the level of work stress by demographic factors (gender, status, education qualification, job position and length of service). However, the findings showed that only organizational factors have a significant relationship with work stress level. Findings of the study also revealed that the overall level of work stress among respondent is moderate.

Alam & Dilruba (2016), "Job Satisfaction and Job Stress among Bank Employees in Rajshahi City: A Field Study" through their study investigated the job satisfaction and job stress of bank employees in Bangladesh. The sample of the study comprised of respondents selected purposively. Job Satisfaction Scale (Abdul Khaleque, 1995) and Occupation Stress Index (Md. Abdul Latif and Sabina Sultana) were used for data collection. Results of the study revealed that two-third of the participants were satisfied with their jobs and almost one-third of the bank employees had low job stress. The results also showed that there is no significant correlation between job stress and job satisfaction.

Kishori & Vinothini (2016) in their research attempted to evaluate the factors causing stress among banking employees and measure the stress level among banking employees. Descriptive research was conducted for the study with a population of 250 employees. Since stress in the banking sector is mostly due to excess of work pressure and work-life imbalance, the organizations should support and encourage employees taking up roles that will help them to balance work and family. The productivity of the workforce is the most decisive factor as far as the success of an organization is concerned. The productivity, in turn, is dependent on the psychosocial wellbeing of the employees. In an age of the highly dynamic and competitive world, man is exposed to all kinds of stressors that can affect him on all realms of life. The growing importance of interventional strategies is felt more at the organizational level. This particular research was intended to study the impact of occupational stress on Nationalized Bank employees. Although certain limitations were met with the study, every effort has been made to make it much comprehensive.

Shahid et al. (2011) through their study tried to explore the stress-related problems of bankers and examine the relationship between stress and performance. They also attempted to identify the various factors contributing to job stress and the impact of stress on employee performance. Structured questionnaires were used for collecting data. The results of the study showed that all the components of stress cause great stress in bankers and then decrease their performance. Work overload, risky job, and poor co-worker relations were found to be the major contributors to job stress in bankers. It was recommended that proper strategies should be made regarding working hours, interpersonal relationships and supervision of bankers to reduce stress and to better manage the performance of employees in the banking sector.

Lopes & Kachalia (2016) conducted research to explore the stress-related problems of bankers and examine the relationship between stress and performance. They also tried to understand which factor plays a crucial role in creating stress among the employees of private and public banks. Being an exploratory design, both primary and secondary data were collected and analyzed through various variables. The results of the study clearly stated that there is a significant relationship between the type of bank, gender, age, education, job role, interpersonal relationships and impact of occupational stress. Therefore, it was recommended that the banking sector employees should adopt new coping strategies for maintaining good physical and mental condition which will improve the productivity level of the bank.

Giorgi et al. (2017) through their study aimed to assess the scale of the phenomenon and how far it related specifically to the processes of bank organization. With this in mind, through a review of the literature, they selected the main studies dealing with work-related stress in banking, so that they could reach a better understanding of the phenomenon as it relates specifically to this set of workers. The study concluded that occupational stress has clearly become a significant cause of ill health and is a serious risk factor for bank workers' psychological and social well-being. This literature review has demonstrated an increasing diffusion of adverse health outcomes from work-related stress in this sector.

Manjunatha & Renukamurthy (2017) in their study found that stress on the job has become the black plague of the present century. The study is based on secondary data. The findings of the study disclosed that the performance of the employee is the most important factor as far as the success of the banking industry is concerned. This, in turn, is dependent on the well-being of the employees. Stress can make an individual productive, constructive and well managed. Positive attitude and meditation will be helpful for coping the stress. There are various ways for managing stress, such as breathing exercises, progressive relaxation, stretching exercise, walking and sleeping. Hence, it will be successful if it makes distress. It enhances the psychological well-being and health of the employees.

To analyze the epidemiology of stress on bank workers, *Mannocci et al. (2018)* conducted a study. This study investigated for the first time the association between occupational stress level in bank-employees using the BEST8, Karasek-Model and socio-demographic and working factors in Italy. It was found that the workers more stressed were older with a commercial role and consumer of antidepressants/sedatives. The study concluded that the occupational stress level in the banking sector involves many aspects: gender, type of bank, role, personal morals, high job demands, low level of decision-making. This study recommended that banks should implement strategic interventions for the well-being of employees, and consequently for their productivity.

Dhankar (2015), "Occupational Stress in Banking Sector" attempted to find out the stress level among banking employees and understand which factor plays a crucial role for creating stress among the employees of private and public banks. It was concluded from the study that there is not a single factor which determines the stress in banking employees. Factors like work overload, ambiguity, pressure, confliction, etc. are responsible for stress. Occupational stress has become a leading feature of modern life. It has wide-ranging effects on employees' behavior. A substantial portion of organization research involves the study of stress among employees. A large number of problems related to employee health, declining levels of productivity and competence are related to occupational stress. Minimizing occupational stress in the coming time would be a part of the company policy of the organizations and be seen as an imperative strategy to target better employee satisfaction.

3.3.3 REVIEW OF LITERATURE RELATED WITH CONSEQUENCES OF STRESS

Ivona Vrdoljak Raguž & Ivana Čučuk. (2015) presented the managerial stress among managers and subordinates. The study elucidated that some amount of stress can be effective in the work performance of an individual, but the problem arises when the amount of stress exceeds a certain critical point and leads to the burnout syndrome, whose victims are mostly managers. The roles of managers, their skills, functions and modern management trends are determinants of every manager's job from which various stressors arises, i.e. sources of stress at work. The study revealed that stress management should become one of the business philosophies of every business. Stress produces not only losses for the individual and his family but also for the organization itself because it causes great financial losses. Consequently, it is essential for each organization to discover, develop and preserve unique programs, strategies and stress management methods by applying them to all employees.

The study by **Donovan et al. (2013)** shows that stress is an important issue within nursing and it is difficult to find agreement among those who are expert in the area regarding a concise definition of stress. The objective of the research was to identify and discuss the effect of stress on health and its relationship to nursing. The study revealed that addressing these issues in nursing practice will involve employers acknowledging their responsibility and mandating work-rest schedules be instituted into healthcare facilities, as self-regulation fails to provide sufficient breaks to guard against physiological strain.

Mawanza (2017) conducted a research study with the objective of evaluating stress and its effect on employees' productivity and managerial responsibility in companies in Zimbabwe. This was motivated by the state of the socio-economic and political affair of the country which seemed to be on a recessionary trend and hence bring in with it a lot of problems and stress to employees and employers. The results of the study showed that change factors, demands or pressure factors, lack of support and participation at work by supervisors and other staff members, and work role were to a greater extent the most stressful factors. The perennial economic crisis in the country, a high degree of uncertainty due to restructurings and redundancies, and work changes without consultations had a positive impact on employee's productivity. The regression results concluded that poor work relationships, lack of support at work, and poor planning had negatively affected productivity.

Toussaint et al. (2016), "Effects of lifetime stress exposure on mental and physical health in young adulthood: How stress degrades and forgiveness protects health" examined risk and resilience factors that affect health. The study revealed that greater lifetime stress severity and lower levels of forgiveness, each uniquely predicted worse mental and physical health. Analyses also revealed a graded Stress ×

Forgiveness interaction effect, wherein associations between stress and mental health were weaker for persons exhibiting more forgiveness. The study elucidated the interactive effects of cumulative stress severity and forgiveness on health and suggested that developing a more forgiving coping style may help minimize stress-related disorders.

In the study conducted by ***Goswami (2015)*** the impact of occupational stress on employees' performance in banks was evaluated. The sample was collected from banks of major cities of Rajasthan State. Relevant data were collected through a structured questionnaire. The results of the study showed that occupational stress brings about subjective effects such as fear, anger, and anxiety among employees resulting in poor mental and psychological health. Based on these findings, it was recommended that banks should reduce psychological strain, job insecurity, and clear role ambiguity, through job redesign. Other support activities such as behavioral and psychological counseling and short-term courses on time management and workshops on stress management can be organized.

The study by ***Mabiza et al. (2017)*** intended to explore the impacts of operational activities and job performance demand in relation to stress on employees in the banking sector. The specific objectives of the study were therefore stated as, to survey the operational management activities of two selected banks in Johannesburg; to examine the nature of occupational stress in South African banking sector; to investigate the effects of occupational stress on employees' performance in banking in South Africa and, to identify the major stressors in the employees in those banks. The study revealed that the management needs to ensure that a positive atmosphere is created and the employees must cultivate positive attitudes. This view reflects the position of work stress as "residing neither solely in the individual nor in the environment but in the transaction between the two".

Bature et al. (2016) investigated the effects of stress on employees' performance in the United Bank for Africa Plc, Garki Branch. A survey design using the stratified random sampling method that grouped the population into managers and non-managers was adopted for the study. Results of the study showed that excessive overtime, long absence from family, fear of job insecurity and difficult customers were the major stressors in the sampled bank. The study also revealed that the effects of stress on employees' performance existed in the form of mental tiredness, high blood pressure and increased use of medication. Thus, it was recommended that stress management should be enhanced in terms of regular training, openness and understanding among the employees. Also, jobs should be redesigned to reduce workload and role conflict.

Rizwan et al. (2014), "Investigating the Causes of Job Stress: A Study on Banking Sector of Bahawalpur, Pakistan" carried out the study to explore the relationship of job stress with variables such as role conflict, role ambiguity, work overload, and work-family conflict. The study was descriptive in nature and questionnaire method was used for data collection. It was concluded from the research that the relationship between role ambiguity and job stress is null, while role conflict, work overload, and work-family conflict have a significant positive relationship with job stress.

3.3.4 REVIEW OF LITERATURE RELATED WITH COPING METHODS OF JOB STRESS

The study undertaken by *Gyan & Baffoe (2014)* adopted a mixed method to investigate the nature of stress and the coping strategies adopted by bankers in the Tema Metropolis. Data for the study were collected from the field using interview schedules and questionnaires. Findings from the study show the existence of a high level of stress among bankers. The sources of stress among the bankers range from the upbringing of their children, their families to the nature of their work. In terms of coping strategies of stress, it was revealed that the respondents indulge in religious activities, exercises, share with friends, use medicinal therapies, counseling and social gathering. The need for appropriate mechanisms to be put in place by the managements of the banks to address the counseling needs of employees was indicated by the findings. Also, the organization of seminars for employees to help broaden their minds on stress coping strategies as well as to keep them abreast with the changing trend of issues is very essential to help reduce their stress levels.

Enekwe et al. (2014) through their research work tried to investigate the stress management techniques of bank employees in the Nigerian banking industry. They also attempted to find out the relationship between female and male coping mechanisms during stress. The result shows that male and female bank employees will not significantly cope with stress management techniques in the Nigerian banking industry. It also shows that male and female bankers were found not to differ significantly on their stress management technique and that stress management is not gender sensitive or gender-centric. The researcher recommends training, total computerization and various other techniques to enable bank employees' cope-up with the stress in the workplaces. Also, the stress management techniques work best when they are used regularly, not just when the pressure is on knowing how to de-stress and doing it when things are relatively calm can help one get through challenging circumstance that may arise.

Stephen (2014) tried to examine different forms of coping strategies adopted by female employees of commercial banks in Akwa Ibom State, South-South, Nigeria. The cross-sectional descriptive survey design was adopted and various coping strategies as they influence occupational stress were examined. Occupational stress and coping strategy questionnaire were used in data collection. The results of the study revealed that annual leave and getting assistance from colleagues were the most widely used organizational and personal coping strategies, respectively as they significantly reduced occupational stress while lunch breaks and listening to music while on duty were insignificant. Therefore, there is a need for management in commercial banks to increase the level of social support among female employees. Also, sporting/ games facilities such as gym, chess, scrabble, creche, restaurant, staff bus, and staff quarters should be provided for use by employees so as to assist them to cope with occupational stress.

Priya (2017) in her study aimed to identify the stress coping mechanisms adopted by both private and public sector banking employees for downsizing the stress. The findings indicated that there are eight coping dimensions/mechanisms used by both private and public sector banking employees. These are- Time management, Physical relaxation, Entertainment, Optimistic approach, Adequate rest, Temporary relaxation, Diversion, and Decentralization. Results of the study further revealed that private and public sector banks significantly differ in coping dimensions.

The study carried out by *Majumdar and Ray (2010)* explores the general stressors as perceived by the first year postgraduate students of Physical Sciences as well as Social Sciences in the different aspects of post-graduate education, covering the domains career-related stress, interpersonal relationships, expectation from self and others, stress from emerging challenges and time management, as well as their coping strategies. The results of the study reflect important insights into the nature of stress faced by the University students and the ways they try to deal with the same. The study revealed that students reported being assailed by mostly psychological consequences of stress such as tension, anxiety, worry, temper tantrums and hopelessness. It was found that most students reported employing problem-focused coping to deal with stress. Therefore, several interventions were suggested to bring improvements in the current scenario.

The research by *Anbazhagan & Rajan (2013)* reviews and summarizes three decades of empirical literature concerned with stress in general and occupational stress in particular with major coping strategies. The results of the study showed that there are a number of factors which cause occupational stress among executives, supervisors and all other forms of employees based on the intensity of the job and organizational culture. These factors have a high level and a huge impact on employee efficiency. These factors are present in all types of industry, but more in the private industry as there is cut-throat competition and job insecurity issues. These stressors could be managed well in a proper and scheduled manner. But the use of these will depend upon the situation and the nature of the work and employee.

The article presented by *Naseem & Khalid (2010)* reviews the literature on positive thinking and its effect on the appraisal of stress, coping and health outcomes. Positive psychology is a new dimension that focuses on positive thinking, positive emotions and positive behavioral qualities that enhance the human potential in various domains such as work, coping with stress and health. The results of this review can be replicated in Pakistan where negativity due to illiteracy and poverty is prevailing everywhere. Geopolitical situations in the country are alarming and people are under constant strains of bomb blasts. In these circumstances, there should be measures to protect them from negativity. There are implications for educationists who wish to reduce the stressors of their students by preparing them to face the challenges of teaching-learning situations and professional life.

A comparative analysis among Women and Men CBSE affiliated school teachers was carried out by *Prasad et al. (2016)* to assess the occupational stress, coping strategies and its effect on teacher performance. The aim of this research was to study the impact of occupational stress on employee performance at the workplace. It was concluded from the study that medium level stress exists in the workplace of school teachers. The results also indicated that coping strategies are one of the methods to fight stress. These issues need to be addressed by the management of the school by Ergonomics to understand the interactions among humans and other elements of a system, and the profession that applies theory, principles, data, and methods to design in order to optimize human well-being and overall system performance. It was recommended that to avoid role conflict proper strategies need to be developed considering working on flexible hours, interpersonal relationship and supervision and participation of the employees in the stress management may be helpful in coping with the stressors.

3.4 RESEARCH GAP

Job stress and its disastrous consequences have been observed in all the sectors, industries and organizations. One such industry is the banking industry. Although a lot of studies have been undertaken on job stress in different sectors, there are very few studies conducted in the banking sector and that too covering the entire state of Haryana. Today, banking is a fast growing service industry and thus high staff morale is very essential for dealing with the customers effectively and positively. Hence, this study aims to identify and suggest solutions to specific problems related to job stress faced by bank employees.

In this backdrop, the present researcher has been promoted to do research on *"Job Stress Among Employees of Banking Industry (A Comparative Study of Selected Public and Private Sector Banks in Haryana)"*

3.5 SIGNIFICANCE OF THE STUDY

In today's competitive environment there are a number of reasons which indicate that people working in the banking sector are significantly more prone to the risk of poor health because the jobs in the banking industry are becoming more and more stressful. This study will help us to identify the level of stress experienced by employees and major factors causing stress. It will help the top management in adopting the appropriate techniques for stress reduction and also to reduce the labor turnover and absenteeism of employees.

3.6 STATEMENT OF PROBLEM

Stress is caused by an imbalance between the demands upon an individual and the ability to cope with those demands. The demands are perceived as challenges which may arise from either external or internal sources. Individuals have their own personal beliefs that influence their attitudes and actions against such perceived or real threats. In other words, it is apparent that individuals differ from each other in their responses to stressful events in their lives.

Organizational stressors are factors in the workplace that can cause stress. The four general sets of organizational stressors are task demands, physical demands, role demands, and interpersonal demands. Stress-related problems include mood disturbance, psychological distress, sleep disturbance, upset stomach, headache, and problems in relationships with family and friends. The effects of job stress on chronic diseases are more difficult to ascertain because chronic diseases develop over relatively long periods of time and are influenced by many factors other than stress. Nonetheless, there is some evidence that stress plays a role in the development of several types of chronic health problems including cardiovascular disease, musculoskeletal disorders, and psychological disorders.

Banks are considered to be the nerve centre of an economy and the barometer of its economic perspective. The Indian banking structure consists of a heterogeneous mix of indigenous banks, the public sector and private sector commercial banks, new generation banks, foreign banks at base layers, the highly developed State Bank of India at its middle layer, and the State-owned Central Bank 'The Reserve Bank of India' at the apex.

Liberalization, deregulation and global integration of banking activities have increased the risk of the banking industry. Now banks are proactively devising their internal mechanism to withstand these risks. Banks are now rationalizing their branch network by shifting, merging, and closing down the non-viable branches. They have introduced mass computerization with the twin objectives of handling the increased volume of business effectively on the one hand and improving the housekeeping and customer services on the other. Nationalized banks introduced the scheme of voluntary retirement to manage the surplus manpower left due to computerization. Now banks are facing severe competition. They are rationalizing the interest rate and service charges, on the one hand, and becoming more customer-oriented on the other. The increasing competition and shrinking profit margin have led to the voluntary merger of the banks for gaining a competitive edge. Banker-customer contact is reduced to the bare minimum and much of the business is taken over by electronic banking, telebanking and card banking. It can be called 'Anywhere-Anytime Banking'. Banks will become the delivery channel for a host of financial products and services like the insurance, hire purchase and leasing, brokering and consultancy.

As a result of all these changes in the banking industry, life in the organization has become highly stressful. Stress leads to physical disorders because the internal body system changes while trying to cope with stress.

Stress over a long period of time leads to diseases of the heart and other parts of the body system. Therefore, it is important that stress, both on and off the job, must be kept at a low level so that most people may be able to tolerate stress without developing either emotional or physical disorders.

Thus, the study is taken up to explore*"Job Stress Among Employees of Banking Industry [A Comparative Study of Selected Public and Private Sector Banks in Haryana]"*

3.7 OBJECTIVES OF THE STUDY

The proposed research work endeavors to undertake an in-depth study of job stress among the employees of the banking industry. The objectives of the study are:

1. To study and compare the level of job stress among the employees of public and private sector banks.

2. Exploration of various factors which have the potential to produce/cause stress.

3. To compare the level of job stress experienced by male and female employees in the banks under study.

4. To study the effects of stress on employee job satisfaction.

5. To analyze the effects of stress on the health of employees.

6. To identify and compare the various stress coping methods used by public and private sector banks.

3.8 HYPOTHESIS

A supposition; a proposition or principle which is supposed or taken for granted, in order to draw a conclusion or inference for proof of the point in question; something not proved, but assumed for the purpose of argument, or to account for a fact or an occurrence; as, the hypothesis that headwinds detain an overdue steamer. A hypothesis being a mere supposition, there are no other limits to hypotheses than those of the human imagination(J.S.Mill).

The following hypothesis has been formulated for the current research study:

1. H_0: There is no significant difference between the level of stress experienced by the employees of public and private sector banks.

2. H_1: There is a significant difference between the level of stress experienced by the employees of public and private sector banks.

3. H_0: There is no significant difference between the level of stress experienced by male and female employees.

4. H_1: There is a significant difference between the level of stress experienced by male and female employees.

5. H_0: There is no significant difference between the stress coping methods used by public and private sector banks.

6. H_1: There is a significant difference between the stress coping methods used by public and private sector banks.

3.9 SCOPE OF THE STUDY

The present study is conducted to analyze the level of stress experienced by employees working in the banking industry (both public and private). The results of this study will be helpful in understanding the type of factors and job conditions that lead to stress and also the various methods used to cope with stress. The results of the study would also help the policymakers to draw up new policies to manage the problems of job stress in bank employees

The scope of this research study is as under:

- **FUNCTIONAL SCOPE**

The functional scope of this study is to analyze job stress among employees of the Indian banking industry.

- **GEOGRAPHICAL SCOPE**

In this study researcher selected 4 banks (2 Public Sector Banks and 2 Private Sector Banks), which are providing services in India. The Haryana State of India is the geographical criteria for this research study.

3.10 RESEARCH DESIGN

When we talk research methodology, we not only talk of research methods but also consider the logic behind the methods we use in the research study and try to explain why we are using a particular method or technique and why we are not using the other, so that research results are evaluated by the researcher himself or by others. **In short, research methodology consists of these steps:**

Defining the research objective	Developing the research plan	Collecting the information	Analyzing the information	Presenting the findings

The research design is the conceptual structure within which research is conducted; it constitutes the blueprint for the collection, measurement, and analysis of data. This research is an **Exploratory and Descriptive research** study.

3.11 POPULATION OF THE STUDY

The population selected for this particular study comprises of the employees (of all departments) working in various branches of ***Public and Private sector banks of Haryana.***

(a) Selected Public Sector banks of Haryana

- State bank of India
- Union Bank of India

(b)Selected Private Sector banks of Haryana

- HDFC Bank
- ICICI Bank

3.12 SAMPLE DESIGN

Convenience sampling was applied to gather the data. Approximately 1000 questionnaires were administered for the research purpose.

- **Sample frame**: Employees of Banks under study

- **Sample unit**: Public and Private Sector Banks of Haryana

- **Universe**: It means to develop sample design which defines a set of objectives.

Proposed Research consists of all the banks.

- **Sample size:** It refers to the number of items to be selected from the universe to constitute a sample. This Proposed Research Study consists of **some selected public and private sector banks of Haryana.**

- **Method of sampling:** The **Random and Convenience sampling** technique is used in selecting the items for the sample.

- **Sample Size Calculator (Net sample size calculation):**

  This calculator gives out the number of sampling/observation needed for a measurement based on the requirements.

- **Find Out Sample Size:**

  Confidence Level: 95%, level of significance=5%. (Error)

  Confidence Interval:5%

  Population Size: Leave blank if unlimited population size

  Result: Required to measure **385** or more samples. (From one type of bank)

- **Confidence Interval:** In statistics, a confidence interval is a particular kind of interval estimate of a population parameter. During statistical research process instead of estimating the parameter by a single value, a confidence interval is likely to include the parameter or range for e.g. 40±2 or 40±5%.

- **Confidence Level:** Also called the confidence coefficient, confidence level represents the possibility that the confidence interval is to contain the parameter. e.g. 95% confidence level.

- **Population Size:** In statistics, the population is the entire entities concerning which statistical inferences are to be drawn. The population size is the total number of the entire entities.

A sample size of 800 respondents will be taken from the four banks in Haryana, comprising:

TABLE 3.1 SAMPLE FRAME OF RESPONDENTS

S. No	Bank	No. of Respondents (Employees)
PUBLIC SECTOR BANK		
1	State Bank of India	200
2	Union Bank of India	200
PRIVATE SECTOR BANK		
3	HDFC Bank	200
4	ICICI Bank	200
TOTAL		800

3.13 PERIOD OF THE STUDY

This research study covered the data of last five years of the functioning of the selected banks. A longer period can be selected but due to time and resource constraints, the last five years have been taken for analyzing the data of the research program. The study period was 5 years, starting from the year 2011-12 to 2015-16.

3.14 NATURE OF THE STUDY

Descriptive, exploratory and analytical research design is used in the current research study, which employs facts or information to be collected from the primary source and also illustrates already available information, and analyze them to make a critical evaluation of the subject. Basically, the analytical part utilized the statistical inputs and verified the research hypothesis put forward in the study.

3.15 DATA COLLECTION DESIGN

To make the findings of this research more reliable and valid, this research has utilized both primary and secondary data.

- **PRIMARY DATA:** A standard and structured questionnaire was used to collect the primary data for the study and the entire state of Haryana will be covered for the collection of data.

- **SECONDARY DATA:** To achieve the stated objectives, data was collected from various sources such as RBI website, Indian Banks Association, Annual reports of IRDA, various textbooks of banking, books on Income of Banks, Insurance magazines, newspaper, journals, banks annual reports and newspapers, publications, official websites, etc.

3.16 ANALYSIS & INTERPRETATION OF DATA

The collected primary and secondary data for the study were summarized and tabulated. Bar diagram and graphs are used at the appropriate places to present and classify the available data. Charts were used to simplify the data for analytical purpose. In order to analyze stress related issues of bank employees of selected banks, the following tools were used:

3.17 STATISTICAL TOOLS AND TECHNIQUES

Descriptive Analysis: Statistical methods were used to summarize or describe the collection of data. Various descriptive statistical tools such as frequencies, charts and graphs, percentages, arithmetic averages, correlation, and standard deviations, etc. were used according to the data.

Influential Analysis:

Classification, presentation and analysis of data: The researcher has to classify the raw data into some purposeful and usable categories. Tabulation is a part of the technical procedure wherein the classified data is put in the form of tables. Analysis work after tabulation is generally based on the computation of various percentages, ratios, and coefficient, etc by applying various well-defined formulae. In the process of analysis, relationships or differences, supporting or conflicting with the original hypothesis should determine with what validity data can be said to indicate conclusion.

TOOLS FOR TESTING HYPOTHESIS:

The data collected from the questionnaire was used to check the hypothesis. For hypothesis testing, the following statistical techniques have been used on the tabulated data.

- **Normality test**

To check the reliability of the questionnaire Normality test (Cronbach's Alpha) has been applied with the help of SPSS software.

- **Likert's Scale**

Depending on the requirement of scaling/ranking for questionnaire Four Point/ Five Point Likert's scale has been applied on various questions and score sheet was formulated.

- **t' Test**

A *t*-test is any statistical hypothesis test in which the test statistic follows a Student's *t* distribution if the null hypothesis is true. It is most commonly applied when the test statistic would follow a normal distribution if the value of a scaling term in the test statistic were known. When the scaling term is unknown and is replaced by an estimate based on the data, the test statistics (under certain conditions) follows a Student's hypothesis that the population mean is equal to a specified value the statistic,

$$ t = \frac{\overline{x} - \mu_0}{s / \sqrt{n}} , $$

Where '*s*' is the sample standard deviation and '*n*' is the sample size. The degrees of freedom used in this test is regression coefficients and if it is greater than the table 't' value, we reject the null hypothesis other-wise we accept it at various levels of significance.

- **ANOVA**

ANOVA measures two sources of variation in the data and compares their relative sizes variation.

➤ Variation BETWEEN groups, for each data value look at the difference between its group mean and the overall mean

$$\left(\overline{x}_i - \overline{x}\right)^2$$

➤ Variation WITHIN groups for each data value look at the difference between that value and the mean of its group

$$\left(x_{ij} - \overline{x}_i\right)^2$$

The ANOVA F-statistic is a ratio of the Between Group& the Within Group Variation:

$$F = \frac{Between}{Within} = \frac{MSG}{MSE}$$

A large 'F' is evidence *against* H0 since it indicates that there is more difference between groups than within groups.

Research Methodology is the backbone of research work. We have ascertained various tools, techniques, models and conceptual framework in this chapter. With all these efforts we have comprehended this research work. We have collected primary and secondary data. With the help of SPSS and Microsoft Excel, we have analyzed these data. The results are critically evaluated and described logically in this thesis. All the objectives and hypothesis are studied, analyzed and tested in the following chapters.

1.18 CONTRIBUTION OF THE STUDY

CONTRIBUTION TO THE KNOWLEDGE

1. Through this research study, the knowledge of researcher particularly regarding statistical tools and techniques and statistical tests will improve.

2. The knowledge regarding job stress among employees will be improved.

CONTRIBUTION TO SOCIETY

1. Through this research study, society will be able to know the real situation of job stress of employees in the banks.

2. Customers will be able to take the proper decision regarding the selection of services of the banks.

3. Society will be able to know the various types of banking facilities and services.

CONTRIBUTION TO THE INDUSTRY

1. The banking industry may be able to know the financial efficiency with the help of coping strategies in order to reduce job stress among bank employees.

2. The banking industry will try to improve its facilities and employee standards through this research work.

3.19 LIMITATIONS OF THE STUDY

Even though utmost care was exercised in all aspects of this research, certain limitations have been perceived and came across while conducting the study. The sector is very vast and it was not possible to cover every nook and corner of this sector. Some of the limitations of the study are:

- The study was conducted for the period 2011-12 to 2015-16. Influence of regulatory measures taken after the study period might influence the findings of the study.

- In this study, certain accounting & statistical tools are used e.g. ratios, mean, etc. these tools have their own limitations which also apply to this research work.

- The present study covered two public and two private sector banks. So any generalization for universal application is very difficult and cannot be applied, because the results of this study are confined and limited to the selected banks.

- The study was conducted only in some selected branches of Haryana location.

- The respondent bias would have to some extent affected the quality of data in spite of all precautionary measures taken to ensure its reliability. As there is no possible way the researcher can ensure that the interviewees always understand the true context of each question in the way the researcher wants the interviewees to understand it.

REFERENCES

- Aliah Binti Roslan. (2011). Analysis of Work Stress Among Bank Employees: A Case Study of Bank Rakyat, University Utara Malaysia

- Alice Mannocci. Laura Marchini, Alfredo Scognamiglio , Alessandra Sinopoli , Simone De Sio ID , Sabina Sernia and Giuseppe La Torre. (2018). Are Bank Employees Stressed? Job Perception and Positivity in the Banking Sector: An Italian Observational Study, *International Journal of Environmental Research and Public Health,* Vol. 15

- Anbazhagan & L.J.Soundar Rajan. (2013). A Conceptual Framework of Occupational Stress and Coping Strategies. *ZENITH International Journal of Business Economics & Management Research*, Vol.3 (5)

- Asim Masood. (2013). Effects of Job Stress on Employee Retention: A Study on Banking Sector of Pakistan. *International Journal of Scientific and Research Publications*, Volume 3, Issue 9

- B Kishori & B Vinothini. (2016). Positive Thinking in Coping with Stress and Health outcomes: Literature Review. *Journal of Research and Reflections in Education*, Vol.4, No.1, pp 42 -61

- Bature Nana Usman, Ayuba Aminu & Nathaniel Ozigbo. (2016). Effects of Work Stress on Employees' Performance in United Bank of Africa Plc, Garki Branch, Abuja

- Carol Lopes & Dhara Kachalia. (2016). Impact of Job Stress on Employee Performance in Banking Sector. *International Journal of Science Technology and Management*, Vol. 5, Issue 3

- Charles Gyan & Michael Baffoe. (2014). Stress and Coping Strategies among Bankers in the Tema Metropolis. *Developing Country Studies*, Vol. 4, No. 25

- Chathuni Jayasinghe and M.V.S. Mendis. (2017). Stress and Job performance: A study on banking sector of Northern region of Sri Lanka. *International Journal of Research Publications* Volume 1 – Issue. 1

- Donovan O', R., Doody, O. and Lyons, R. (2013). The effect of stress on health and its implications for nursing. *British Journal of Nursing*, Vol. 22(16), pp: 969-973.

- Enekwe, Chinedu Innocent; Agu, Charles Ikechukwu and Eziedo Kenneth Nnagbogu. (2014). Stress Management Techniques in Banking Sectors in Nigeria. *IOSR Journal of Business and Management*, Volume 16, Issue 7. Ver. IV, pp: 33-38

- Essien, Blessing Stephen. (2014). Occupational Stress and Coping Strategies among Female Employees of Commercial Banks in Nigeria. *International Journal of scientific research and management*, Volume 2, Issue 9, pp: 1417-1430

- Gabriele Giorgi, Gulio Arcangell. Milda Perminiene, Chiara Lohiri. (2017). Work-Related Stress in the Banking Sector: A Review of Incidence, Correlated Factors, and Major Consequences. *Frontiers in Psychology*

- Goswami Tulsee Giri. (2015). Job Stress And Its Effect On Employee Performance In Banking Sector. *Indian Journal of Commerce & Management Studies*, Volume VI Issue 2

- Ibtisam Mbarak Awadh , Lucy Gichinga and Dr. Anwar Hood Ahmed. (2015). Effects of Workplace Stress on Employee Performance in the County Governments in Kenya: A Case Study of Kilifi County Government, *International Journal of Scientific and Research Publications*, Volume 5, Issue 10

- Ivona Vrdoljak Raguž & Ivana Čučuk. (2015). Managerial Stress – Effects and Consequences. *Management and Organisation*

- Jitendar Singh Narban, Bhanu Pratap Singh Narban, Jitendra Singh. (2016). A Conceptual Study on Occupational Stress (Job Stress/Work Stress) and its Impacts. *IJARIIE International Journal*, Vol. 2, Issue1

- Junior Mabiza, Member, IAENG, Joyce Conduah, and Charles Mbohwa. (2017). Occupational Role Stress on Employee Performance and the Resulting Impact: A South African Bank Perspective. *Proceedings of the International MultiConference of Engineers and Computer Scientists*, Vol II, pp: 15 – 17

- M.Kotteeswari & S.Tameem Sharief. (2014). JOB STRESS AND ITS IMPACT ON EMPLOYEES' PERFORMANCE A STUDY WITH REFERENCE TO EMPLOYEES WORKING IN BPOS. *International Journal of Business and Administration Research Review*, Vol.2, Issue.4

- Mai Ngoc Khuong and Vu Hai Yen. (2016). Investigate the Effects of Job Stress on Employee Job Performance — A Case Study at Dong Xuyen Industrial Zone, Vietnam. *International Journal of Trade, Economics and Finance*, Vol. 7, No. 2

- Majumdar Bishakha and Anjali Ray. (2010). Stress and Coping Strategies among University Students: A Phenomenological Study. *Indian Journal Social Science Researches*, Vol. 7, No. 2, pp. 100-111

- Manjunatha M K. & Dr.T.P.Renukamurthy. (2017). Stress Among Banking Employee- A Literature Review. *International Journal of Research Granthaalayah*, Vol.5 (Iss.1)

- Moaz Nagib Gharib, Syed Ahsan Jamil, Moinuddin Ahmed & Suhail Ghouse. (2016). The Impact of Job Stress on Job Performance: A Case Study on Academic Staff at Dhofar University. *International Journal of Economic Research*. Vol. 13(1), pp: 21-33

- Muhammad Naeem Shahid, Khalid Latif, Nadeem Sohail & Muhammad Aleem Ashraf. (2018). Work Stress and Employee Performance in Banking Sector Evidence From District Faisalabad, Pakistan. *Asian Journal of Business and Management* Sciences, Vol. 1 No. 7, pp: 38-47

- Muhammad Riaz, Nazir Ahmad, Maryam Riaz, Ghulam Murtaza, Tayyaba Khan & Hira Firdous. (2016). Impact of Job Stress on Employee Job Satisfaction. *International Review of Management and Business Research,* Vol. 5 Issue.4

- Muhammad Umair Manzoor , Muhammad Usman, Muhammad Akram Naseem, Malik Muhammad Shafiq. (2011). A Study of Job Stress and Job Satisfaction among Universities Faculty in Lahore, Pakistan. *Global Journal of Management and Business Research*, Volume 11 Issue 9

- Naseem K & Khalid Roshan. (2010). Impact of Job Stress on The Performance of The Bank Employees. *International Journal of Science, Environment and Technology,* Vol. 6, No 3, pp: 1843 – 1851

- Naser Hoboubi, Alireza Choobineh, Fatemeh Kamari Ghanavati, Sareh Keshavarzi & Ali Akbar Hosseini. (2017). The Impact of Job Stress and Job Satisfaction on Workforce Productivity in an Iranian Petrochemical Industry, *Safety and Health at Work*, Vol. 8, pp: 67-71

- Prasad KDV Rajesh Vaidya and V Anil Kumar. (2016). Occupational Stress and Coping Strategies Effect on Teacher Performance: A Comparative Analysis among Women and Men Teachers Affiliated to CBSE Schools in and around Hyderabad. *IOSR Journal of Business and Management,* Volume 18, Issue 11. Ver. II, PP 38-50

- Priya R. (2017). Stress Coping Mechanisms adopted by Banking Sector Employees for Downsize the Stress: a Study. *IOSR Journal of Business and Management*, Volume 19, Issue 6. Ver. III, PP 13-17

- R.G.Ratnawat & P.C. Jha (2014). Impact of Job Related Stress on Employee Performance: A Review and Research Agenda. *IOSR Journal of Business and Management*, Volume 16, Issue 11.Ver. V, PP 01-06

- Rizwan Muhammad, Muhammad Ali Raza, Muhammad Abdul Mateen, Faisal Tehseen, Muhammad Shahaid Farooq, Amajad Javed, Sharjeel Javed. (2014). Investigating the Causes of Job Stress: A Study on Banking Sector of Bahawalpur, Pakistan. *International Journal of Learning & Development,* Vol. 4, No. 2

- Sabrina Shajeen Alam & Dilruba. (2016). Job Satisfaction and Job Stress among Bank Employees in Rajshahi City: A Field Study. *The International Journal of Indian Psychology*, Volume 3, Issue 2, No.5

- Sharmilee Bala Murali, Abdul Basit & Zubair Hassan. (2017). Impact of Job Stress on Employee Performance. *International Journal of Accounting & Business Management,* Vol. 5 (No.2)

- Shavita Dhankar. (2015). Occupational stress in banking sector. *International Journal of Applied Research*, Vol. 1(8), pp: 132-135

- Toussaint Loren, Grant S Shields, Gabriel Dorn1 and George M Slavich. (2014). Effects of lifetime stress exposure on mental and physical health in young adulthood: How stress degrades and forgiveness protects health, Journal of Health Psychology,Vol. 21(6) 1004–1014

- Wilford Mawanza. (2017). The Effects of Stress on Employee Productivity: A Perspective of Zimbabwe's Socio-Economic Dynamics of 2016, Journal of Economics and Behavioral Studies, *Economics and Behavioral Studies* (ISSN: 2220-6140) Vol. 9, No. 2, pp. 22-32

CHAPTER-IV

DATA ANALYSIS AND INTERPRETATION

In the previous chapter, literature related to the research study was reviewed and details were provided regarding the research design, instruments used, the rationale behind the pilot questionnaire, sampling method, data collection procedure, description of variables, various tests employed, etc. The current chapter elaborates the data analysis, interpretation and hypotheses testing of current research design.

4.1 INTRODUCTION OF DATA ANALYSIS IN CURRENT RESEARCH

Stress is caused by an imbalance between the demands upon an individual and the ability to cope with those demands. The demands are perceived as challenges which may arise from either external or internal sources. Individuals have their own personal beliefs that influence their attitudes and actions against such perceived or real threats. In other words, it is apparent that individuals differ from each other in their responses to stressful events in their lives.

Organizational stressors are factors in the workplace that can cause stress. The four general sets of organizational stressors are task demands, physical demands, role demands, and interpersonal demands. Stress-related problems include mood disturbance, psychological distress, sleep disturbance, upset stomach, headache and problems in relationships with family and friends. The effects of job stress on chronic diseases are more difficult to ascertain because chronic diseases develop over relatively long periods of time and are influenced by many factors other than stress. Nonetheless, there is some evidence that stress plays a role in the development of several types of chronic health problems including cardiovascular disease, musculoskeletal disorders, and psychological disorders.

Banks are considered to be the nerve centre of an economy and the barometer of its economic perspective. The Indian banking structure consists of a heterogeneous mix of indigenous banks, the public sector and private sector commercial banks, new generation banks, foreign banks at base layers, the highly developed State Bank of India at its middle layer and the State-owned Central Bank 'The Reserve Bank of India' at the apex.

Liberalization, deregulation and global integration of banking activities have increased the risk of the banking industry. Now banks are proactively devising their internal mechanism to withstand these risks. Banks are now rationalizing their branch network by shifting, merging and closing down the non-viable branches. They have introduced mass computerization with the twin objectives of handling the increased volume of business effectively on the one hand and improving the housekeeping and customer services on the other. Nationalized banks introduced the scheme of voluntary retirement to manage the surplus manpower left due to computerization. Now banks are facing severe competition. They are rationalizing the interest rate and service charges, on one hand, and becoming more customer-oriented on the other. The increasing competition and shrinking profit margin have led to the voluntary merger of the banks for gaining the competitive edge. Banker-customer contact is reduced to the bare minimum and much of the business is taken over by electronic banking, telebanking and card banking. It can be called 'Anywhere-Anytime Banking'. Banks will become the delivery channel for a host of financial products and services like the insurance, hire purchase and leasing, brokering and consultancy.

As a result of all these changes in the banking industry, life in the organization has become highly stressful. Stress leads to physical disorders because the internal body system changes while trying to cope with stress.

Stress over a long period of time leads to diseases of the heart and other parts of the body system. Therefore, it is important that stress, both on and off the job, must be kept at a low level so that most people may be able to tolerate stress without developing either emotional or physical disorders.

In the current research study, the survey was done on primary data collected through employees of selected Public and Private sector banks working in various bank departments, with the help of questionnaires which were evaluated to comparatively elucidate the ***Job Stress Among Employees of Banking Industry in Public and Private Sector Banks of Haryana.***

The self-administered questionnaires were distributed to 800 Banks employees who are directly or indirectly correlated with the Banking activities in regular day to day life.

Before conducting the investigation the investigator introduced herself and well-versed the respondents that their partaking was enormously anonymous, voluntary and private and gave assurance that they could ask questions if they face with any complexity. *All the respondents were also asked some interview scheduled questions and their views on the topics were discussed and framed into observations.*

There are several response formats or scaling methods. *R.A Likert (1932)* developed a scaling format in which the low end represented a negative/ dissatisfaction answer while the high-end represented a positive or highly satisfied response. In this format the employees were allowed to express the degree of their views or opinions about the specific service or product, the survey was conducted for. This format had no restriction to choose between 'yes' and 'no'.

This section peeped deep into the statistical analysis of the data. After completion of a full-fledged survey with a finalized questionnaire, data was arranged in an orderly fashion in a summary of the spreadsheet, by counting the frequency of responses of each question. The hypotheses had been formulated and tested using SPSS software and the results had been arrived at. The total analysis was carried out by using SPSS 18.1 software package.

Scoring of the tool: For every correct response the score is '1' and for every incorrect response the score counted was '0'. The total score of each respondent for each questionnaire separately was calculated on a percentage basis.

Grading of the score was interpreted as follows:

Score obtained	Grade
>81%	Excellent
61-80%	Good
41-60%	Average
< 40%	Poor

Validity: Validity is defined as "the extent to which (a test) measures what it claims to measure" *(Gregory, 1992)*. A measure is valid if it measures what it is supposed to measure and does so cleanly – without accidentally including other factors. The validity of the content was done using content validity. To assess the content validity, the tool was sent to twenty experts (From Academia and Banking Industry). However, only eleven experts reverted back with comments. After the opinions from experts, the tool was modified appropriately and finalized with inculcating certain discussion with the academic mentoring committee.

4.2 STATISTICAL TESTS EMPLOYED

Various statistical tools and tests used for analysis included validity analysis, reliability analysis, reliability testing, Cronbach's Alpha, Kaiser-Meyer-Olkin measure of sampling adequacy, tabulation of data, descriptive statistics, means, averages, factor analysis, total variance analysis, correlation analysis, regression analysis, crosstab, chi-square tests, probability techniques, etc.

4.2.1 Reliability: Reliability is the degree to which measures are free from error and therefore yield consistent results (i.e. the consistency of a measurement procedure). If a measurement device or procedure consistently assigns the same score to individuals or objects with equal values, the instrument is considered reliable.

Cronbach's Alpha was intended as a measure of internal consistency of items in the questionnaire. It varies between zero and one. The closer alpha was to one, the greater the internal consistency of the items in the questionnaire.

TABLE 4.1 RELIABILITY COEFFICIENTS OF BANK EMPLOYEES

Kind of Respondents	N of items	Cronbach's Alpha
Public Sector banks	67	0.892
Private Sector Banks	67	0.813

Source: Primary Data

The results of the pilot study were carefully studied and necessary changes were incorporated in the questionnaire. The total number of statements in the questionnaire were reduced. Then the final questionnaire was administered to the respondents. The data was collected through the face to face interactions with the respondents on the basis of scheduled meetings.

Inference: Cronbach's alpha test was performed to check the reliability of questions or items. Results of Cronbach's alpha test was found to be 0.892 for public sector bank employees whereas for private sector bank employees it was 0.813. Both the values are higher than 0.75 (Standard value for significance), thus it can be postulated that overall score indicates internal consistency of the items in the formulated questionnaire and can be further analyzed for a framed set of objectives and testing of designed variables hypothesis.

4.3 DEMOGRAPHIC ANALYSIS OF EMPLOYEES OF SELECTED BANKS AS RESPONDENTS

Demographic study means the study of both quantitative and qualitative aspects of the selected human population. Quantitative aspects include composition, age, gender, size and structure of the population. Qualitative aspects are the research specific factors such as bank employee bank details, etc. In the current research study, Haryana is chosen as the universe of study. Employees from various selected Public and Private sector banks of Haryana were analyzed in the research. Demographic details of respondents are analyzed in table statements 1 to 14 below:-

Statement 1: Gender of Respondents

TABLE 4.2 GENDER OF RESPONDENTS

Gender	PUBLIC SECTOR		PRIVATE SECTOR	
	Frequency	Percentage (%)	Frequency	Percentage (%)
Male	261	65.25%	229	57.25%
Female	139	34.75%	171	42.75%

CHART 4.1 GENDER OF RESPONDENTS

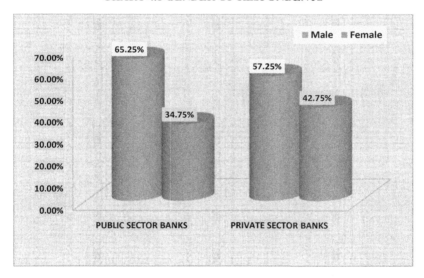

Interpretation:

From the above table, the demographic details of 800 respondents of public (400) and private (400) sector banks can be evaluated. In the first parameter, the gender of respondents was analyzed where a maximum of 65.25% and 57.25% of respondents were male for both public and private sector banks, respectively whereas the remaining 34.75% and 42.75% respondents were females. From the table, it can be concluded that female respondents were more in private sector banks as compared to public sector banks.

Statement 2: Age Group of Respondents

TABLE 4.3 AGE OF RESPONDENTS

Age Group (Years)	PUBLIC SECTOR		PRIVATE SECTOR	
	Frequency	Percentage (%)	Frequency	Percentage (%)
18-28	19	4.75%	251	62.75%
28-38	204	51%	96	24%
38-48	105	26.25%	31	7.75%
Above 48	72	18%	22	5.5%

CHART 4.2 AGE OF RESPONDENTS

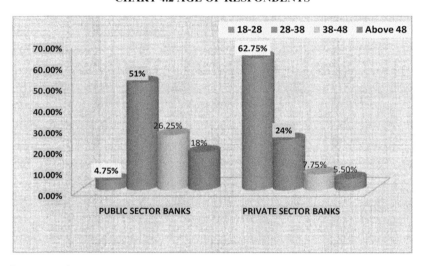

Interpretation:

In this parameter, the age group of banks employees as respondents was evaluated. The maximum respondents i.e. 51% were between the age group of 28 to 38 years of age in public sector banks whereas in private sector banks the maximum respondents i.e. 62.75% were between the age group of 18 to 28 years of age. The minimum respondents i.e. 4.75% of public sector banks were between the age group of 18 to 28 years whereas the minimum respondents i.e. 5.5% of private sector banks were above the age of 48 years. It can be analyzed from the table that maximum respondents of public sector banks were having more age as compared to the private sector banks.

Statement 3: Designation of Respondents

TABLE 4.4 DESIGNATION OF RESPONDENTS

Designation	PUBLIC SECTOR		PRIVATE SECTOR	
	Frequency	Percentage (%)	Frequency	Percentage (%)
Office Assistant	98	24.5%	101	25.25%
Cashiers	152	38%	127	31.75%
Manager	103	25.75%	111	27.75%
Senior Manager	47	11.75%	61	15.25%

CHART 4.3 DESIGNATION OF RESPONDENTS

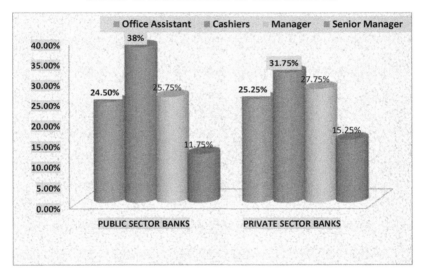

Interpretation:

In this parameter, the designation of respondents was analyzed for public and private sector banks. Maximum respondents i.e. 38% and 31.75% for both public and private sector banks were cashiers whereas the minimum respondents i.e. 11.75% and 15.25% were senior managers in public and private sector banks, respectively. The remaining 24.5% and 25.25% respondents were office assistants in both the banks whereas 25.75% and 27.75% respondents were managers in public and private sector banks, respectively as shown in the above table.

Statement 4: Department of Respondents

TABLE 4.5 DEPARTMENT OF RESPONDENTS

Department	PUBLIC SECTOR		PRIVATE SECTOR	
	Frequency	Percentage (%)	Frequency	Percentage (%)
Loan	101	25.25%	187	46.75%
Cash	163	40.75%	116	29%
IT	49	12.25%	56	14%
Insurance	87	21.75%	41	10.25%

CHART 4.4 DEPARTMENT OF RESPONDENTS

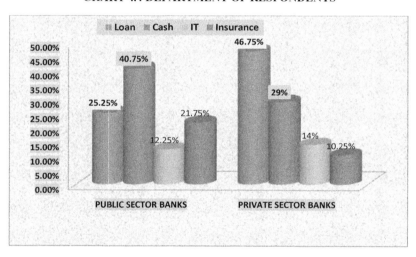

Interpretation:

Another significant demographic parameter was the department in which the respondents of public and private sector banks were working. It was revealed that maximum respondents i.e. 40.75% of public sector banks were working in the cash department whereas 46.75% of respondents of private sector banks were working in the loan department. The minimum respondents i.e. 12.25% of public sector banks were working in the IT department whereas 10.25% of respondents of private sector banks were working in the insurance department. The rest 25.25% of respondents of public sector banks were working in the loan department whereas 29% of private sector respondents were working in the cash department.

111

Statement 5: Experience of Respondents

TABLE 4.6 EXPERIENCE OF RESPONDENTS

Total Experience	PUBLIC SECTOR		PRIVATE SECTOR	
(in years)	Frequency	Percentage (%)	Frequency	Percentage (%)
Less than 1 year	65	16.25%	109	34%
1-3 years	118	29.5%	136	27.25%
4-5 years	129	32.25%	91	22.75%
More than 5 years	88	22%	64	16%

CHART 4.5 EXPERIENCE OF RESPONDENTS

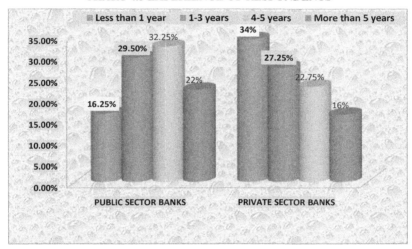

Interpretation:

This parameter evaluates the total experience of respondents from public and private sector banks. The maximum respondents i.e. 32.25% from public sector banks were having a total experience of 4 to 5 years whereas in private sector banks 34% of respondents were having an experience of less than 1 year. The minimum respondents of public sector banks i.e. 16.25% were having less than 1-year experience whereas in private sector banks the minimum respondents i.e. 16% were having more than 5 years of experience. The remaining 29.50% respondents were having 1 to 3 years of experience and 22% were having more than 5 years of experience in public sector banks. In the case of private sector banks, 27.25% of respondents were having 1 to 3 years of experience and the remaining 22.75% of the respondents were having 4 to 5 years of experience in total.

Statement 6: Present Position Experience of Respondents

TABLE 4.7 PRESENT POSITION EXPERIENCE OF RESPONDENTS

Experience (In years) (at present position)	PUBLIC SECTOR		PRIVATE SECTOR	
	Frequency	Percentage (%)	Frequency	Percentage (%)
Less than 1 year	147	36.75%	174	43.5%
1-3 years	116	29%	145	36.25%
4-5 years	98	24.5%	52	13%
More than 5 years	39	9.75%	29	7.25%

CHART 4.6 PRESENT POSITION EXPERIENCE OF RESPONDENTS

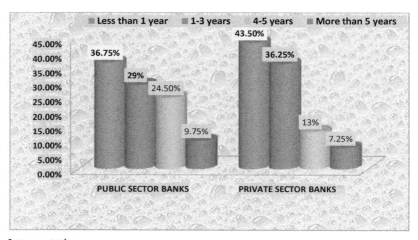

Interpretation:

Another significant demographic parameter was the experience level of employees of public and private sector banks in the present position. Maximum respondents i.e. 36.75% of public sector banks and 43.5% of private sector banks were having less than 1 year of experience at their present position whereas the minimum respondents i.e. 9.75% and 7.25% of both the public and private sector banks were having more than 5 years of experience at their present position, respectively. The remaining 29% and 36.25% respondents of both banks were having experience between 1 to 3 years whereas 24.5% and 13% respondents of public and private sector banks were having 4 to 5 years of experience at present position, respectively.

Statement 7: Qualification of Respondents

TABLE 4.8 QUALIFICATIONS OF RESPONDENTS

Qualification	PUBLIC SECTOR		PRIVATE SECTOR	
	Frequency	Percentage (%)	Frequency	Percentage (%)
10th	36	9%	35	8.75%
12th	49	12.25%	73	18.25%
Graduate	103	25.75%	155	38.75%
Post Graduate	171	42.75%	99	24.75%
Others	41	10.25%	38	9.5%

CHART 4.7 QUALIFICATIONS OF RESPONDENTS

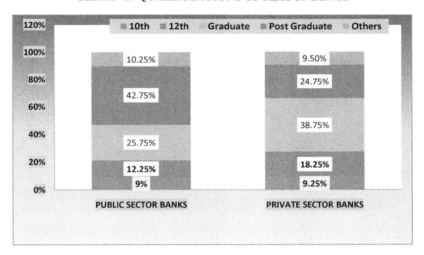

Interpretation:

In this demographic parameter, the qualification of respondents has been analyzed. The maximum respondents in public sector banks i.e. 42.75% were post graduates whereas the maximum respondents from the private sector banks i.e. 38.75% were graduates. The minimum respondents of both the banks (9% and 8.75%) were 10th pass students. The remaining 12.25% and 18.25% respondents were 12th pass in both the banks whereas 10.25% and 9.5% respondents from both the banks were categorized in others.

Statement 8: Annual Salary of Respondents

TABLE 4.9 ANNUAL SALARY OF RESPONDENTS

Annual Salary	PUBLIC SECTOR		PRIVATE SECTOR	
	Frequency	Percentage (%)	Frequency	Percentage (%)
2 to 5 lacs	199	49.75%	262	65.5%
5 to 8 lacs	81	20.25%	58	14.5%
8 to 10 lacs	52	13%	44	11%
10 lacs and above	68	17%	36	9%

CHART 4.8 ANNUAL SALARY OF RESPONDENTS

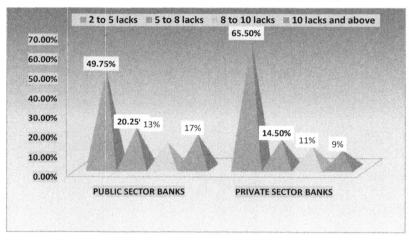

Interpretation:

In the above parameter, the annual salary of the respondents from public and private sector banks was analyzed. The maximum respondents of both public and private sector banks i.e. 49.75% and 65.5% respectively, were having an annual income of 2 to 5 lacs whereas the minimum respondents i.e. 13% of public sector banks were having annual income of 8 to 10 lacs and in private sector banks 9% of the respondents were getting more than 10 lacs annually. The remaining 20.25% respondents of public sector banks and 14.5% respondents of private sector banks were having an annual income between 5 to 8 lacs. The rest 17% respondents of public sector banks were getting more than 10 lacs income annually and 11% respondents of private sector banks were having 8 to 10 lacs income annually. Thus, from above it can be concluded that more of private sector bank respondents were having their annual income between 2 to 5 lacs as compared to public sector banks.

Statement 9: Additional Work Responsibility Assigned to Respondents

TABLE 4.10 ADDITIONAL WORK RESPONSIBILITY ASSIGNED TO RESPONDENTS

Additional work responsibility assigned	PUBLIC SECTOR		PRIVATE SECTOR	
	Frequency	Percentage (%)	Frequency	Percentage (%)
Yes	177	44.25%	319	79.75%
No	223	55.75%	81	20.25%

CHART 4.9 ADDITIONAL WORK RESPONSIBILITY ASSIGNED TO RESPONDENTS

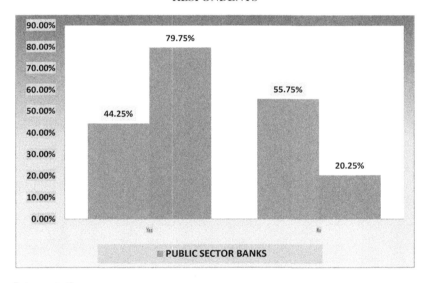

Interpretation:

This parameter analyses the responses of respondents on the basis of additional work responsibility assigned to them. It was disclosed that maximum respondents i.e. 79.75% of private sector banks were assigned additional work whereas only 44.25% of the respondents in public sector banks were assigned additional work. The remaining 55.75% and 20.25% respondents of both the public and private sector banks disagreed, respectively.

Statement 10: Increments or Promotion of Respondents

TABLE 4.11 INCREMENT OR PROMOTION OF RESPONDENTS

Increments/ Promotions received	PUBLIC SECTOR		PRIVATE SECTOR	
	Frequency	Percentage (%)	Frequency	Percentage (%)
Yes	342	85.5%	163	40.75%
No	58	14.5%	237	59.25%

CHART 4.10 INCREMENT OR PROMOTION OF RESPONDENTS

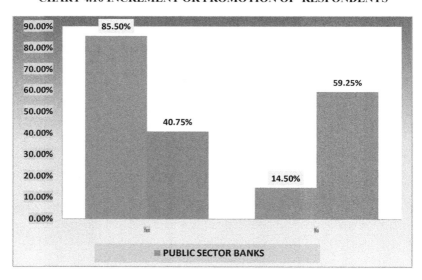

Interpretation:

Another important parameter in the demographic details was the increments received by public and private sector bank employees. Maximum respondents i.e. 85.5% of the public sector banks were receiving increments in comparison to 40.75% respondents of the private sector banks. Only 14.5% of the respondents disagreed from the public sector banks whereas 59.25% of the respondents from private sector banks disagreed to the increment being received.

Statement 11: Marital Status of Respondents

TABLE 4.12 MARITAL STATUS OF RESPONDENTS

Marital Status	PUBLIC SECTOR		PRIVATE SECTOR	
	Frequency	Percentage (%)	Frequency	Percentage (%)
Married	284	71%	232	58%
Unmarried	116	29%	168	42%

CHART 4.11 MARITAL STATUS OF RESPONDENTS

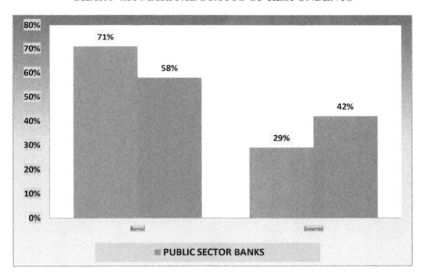

Interpretation:

In this parameter, the marital status of public and private sector respondents was analyzed. The maximum respondents i.e. 71% of public sector banks and 58% of private sector banks were married whereas only 29% and 42% respondents of both the banks, respectively were not married. It can be concluded that more employees of public sector banks were married in comparison to private sector banks.

Statement 12: Family Structure of Respondents

TABLE 4.13 FAMILY STRUCTURE OF RESPONDENTS

Family	PUBLIC SECTOR		PRIVATE SECTOR	
	Frequency	Percentage (%)	Frequency	Percentage (%)
Nuclear	234	58.5%	269	67.25%
Joint	166	41.5%	131	32.75%

CHART 4.12 FAMILY STRUCTURE OF RESPONDENTS

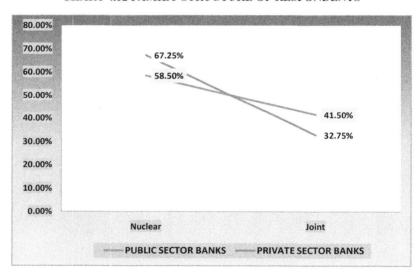

Interpretation:

In the above parameter, the family type of respondents working in public and private sector banks was evaluated. The maximum respondents i.e. 58.5% and 67.25% of both public and private sector banks, respectively were having a nuclear family whereas 41.5% and 32.75% respondents of both the banks were living in a joint family. It can be further noted that more employees from private sector banks were having a nuclear family as compared to public sector bank employees.

Statement 13: Spouse details of Respondents

TABLE 4.14 SPOUSE DETAILS OF RESPONDENTS

If married	PUBLIC SECTOR		PRIVATE SECTOR	
(spouse detail)	Frequency	Percentage (%)	Frequency	Percentage (%)
Working	154	54.23%	178	76.72%
Not working	130	45.77%	54	23.27%

CHART 4.13 SPOUSE DETAILS OF RESPONDENTS

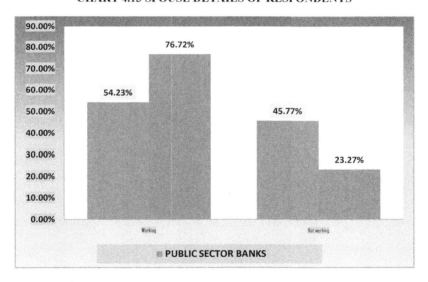

Interpretation:

This parameter analyzes the details of respondents spouse for both public and private sector bank employees. Maximum respondents spouse i.e. 54.23% of public sector banks and 76.72% of private sector banks were working whereas 45.77% and 23.27% of respondents spouse for respective banks were not working. It can be concluded that more respondents spouse from private sector banks were working as compared to public sector banks.

Statement 14: Children details of Respondents

TABLE 4.15 CHILDREN DETAILS OF RESPONDENTS

If married (No. of children)	PUBLIC SECTOR		PRIVATE SECTOR	
	Frequency	Percentage (%)	Frequency	Percentage (%)
0	88	30.98%	102	43.96%
1	145	37.76%	97	41.81%
2	46	16.19%	33	14.12%

CHART 4.14 CHILDREN DETAILS OF RESPONDENTS

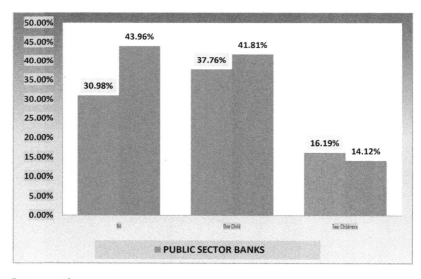

Interpretation:

In the last demographic parameter, the number of children a married respondent had was analyzed. In public sector banks, maximum respondents i.e. 37.76% were having one child whereas in private sector banks, maximum respondents i.e. 43.96% were having no children. The minimum respondents i.e. 16.19% and 14.12% of both the public and private sector banks had two children, respectively.

4.4 CORRELATION PARAMETERS OF WORK AND JOB STRESS

No single factor alone creates job stress among banking employees. Factors like the overload of work, poor working condition, role conflict, role ambiguity, performance pressure, job security, lack of superior support and technological problem are contributing their considerable share in this respect.

Most of the factors associated with the work of bank employees create directly or indirectly stress among bank employees. Thus, the correlation between work and bank employee stress is analyzed in various tables below:

Statement 15:- Mention the number of hours you work for a bank in one day.

TABLE 4.16 WORKING HOURS OF RESPONDENTS IN BANK

Working Hours	Public Sector		Private Sector	
	Frequency	Percentage (%)	Frequency	Percentage (%)
Less than 5 Hours	98	24.5%	52	13%
5 to 8 Hours	223	55.75%	91	22.75%
8 to 12 hours	53	13.25%	203	50.75%
More than 15 hours	26	6.5%	54	13.5%

CHART 4.15 WORKING HOURS OF RESPONDENTS IN BANK

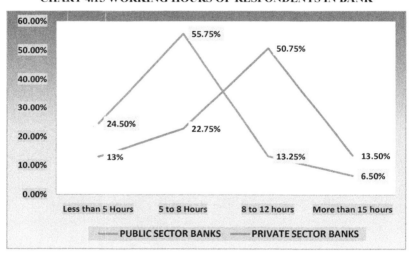

Interpretation:

The above table evaluates the correlation parameters of work and job stress related to public and private sector bank employees. In the first statement, the working hours of public and private sector respondents were analyzed in which maximum respondents i.e. 55.75% of public sector banks were working for 5 to 8 hours a day whereas in private sector banks the maximum respondents i.e. 50.75% were working for 8 to 12 hours a day. The minimum respondents i.e. 6.5% in public sector banks were working more than 15 hours a day whereas in private sector banks the minimum respondents i.e. 13% were working less than 5 hours a day. From the above table, it was revealed that working hours were more in private sector banks than public sector banks.

Statement 16:- Do you suffer from any of the stress-related diseases.

TABLE 4.17 STRESS RELATED DISEASE OF RESPONDENTS

Stress-related disease	Public Sector		Private Sector	
	Frequency	Percentage (%)	Frequency	Percentage (%)
Eyesight problem	65	16.25%	81	20.25%
Obesity	74	18.5%	48	12%
Body Pain	93	23.25%	116	29%
Depression	91	22.75%	96	24%
Any other	77	19.25%	59	14.75%

CHART 4.16 STRESS RELATED DISEASE OF RESPONDENTS

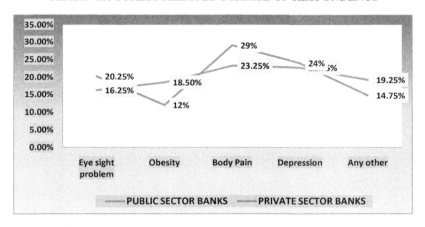

Interpretation:

In the above table, the respondents of public and private sector banks were examined whether they were having any stress related disease or not. The maximum respondents of both public and private sector banks (23.25% and 29%) were suffering from body pain whereas the minimum respondents i.e. 16.25% of public sector banks had eyesight problem and in private sector banks, the minimum respondents i.e. 12% were having the problem of obesity. The remaining 18.5% respondents of public sector banks were having a problem of obesity and 19.25% respondents of public sector banks were having other diseases which are not listed in the table. In respect of the private sector banks, 20.25% respondents were having eyesight problem and 14.75% of respondents were having other diseases which are not listed in the above table.

Statement 17:- Are you managing the Job at Bank and life properly.

TABLE 4.18 MANAGEMENT OF JOB AND LIFE OF RESPONDENTS

Respondents Opinion	Public Sector		Private Sector	
	Frequency	Percentage (%)	Frequency	Percentage (%)
Yes	184	46%	88	22%
No	216	54%	312	78%

CHART 4.17 MANAGEMENT OF JOB AND LIFE OF RESPONDENTS

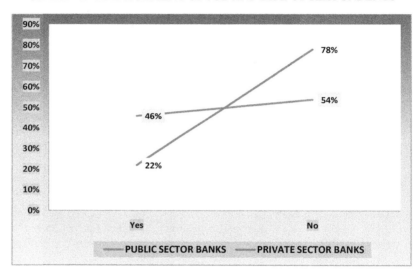

Interpretation:

From the above table, the responses of respondents of public and private sector banks can be analyzed on their management of work and life together. Maximum respondents of both public and private sector banks (54% and 78%) disagreed that they were not able to manage both work & life together whereas 46% respondents from public sector banks and only 22% respondents from private sector banks were able to manage work and life together. Thus, it can be noted that maximum respondents from private sector banks were finding it hard to manage life and work together maybe because of work stress.

Statement 18:- Mention the level of difficulty in managing the work-life balance because of Job Stress.

TABLE 4.19 LEVEL OF WORK-LIFE BALANCE OF RESPONDENTS

Work-Life Balance	Public Sector		Private Sector	
	Frequency	Percentage (%)	Frequency	Percentage (%)
Easy	54	13.5%	55	13.75%
Moderate	205	51.25%	102	25.5%
High	141	35.25%	243	60.75%

CHART 4.18 LEVEL OF WORK-LIFE BALANCE OF RESPONDENTS

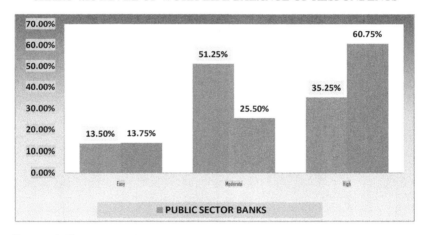

Interpretation:

The above table analyses the level of difficulty faced by public and private sector bank respondents on work and life balance because of job stress. It was found that maximum respondents i.e. 51.25% of public sector banks were having a moderate level of difficulty in managing work-life balance whereas maximum respondents i.e. 60.75% of private sector banks were facing a high level of difficulty in managing work-life balance. The minimum respondents of both the banks i.e. 13.5% and 13.75% were easily managing work-life balance. Only 35.25% respondents from public sector banks were having a high level of difficulty in managing their work-life balance whereas 25.5% respondents of private sector banks were having a moderate level of difficulty in managing work-life balance.

Statement 19:- **Please express how many number of times you exhibit the behavior stated, in a day:**

TABLE 4.20 BEHAVIOUR OF RESPONDENTS IN A DAY

S.no	Statement	RESPONDENTS OPINION					
		Public Sector			Private Sector		
		Never	Sometimes in a day	Always	Never	Sometimes in a day	Always
1.	Angry	125	199	76	68	143	189
2.	Relaxed	143	213	44	201	178	21
3.	Irritable	130	197	73	96	201	103
4.	Exhausted	113	202	85	113	51	236
5.	Satisfied	157	129	114	159	104	137
6.	Depressed	70	224	106	77	183	140
7.	Worthless	127	143	130	203	122	75
8.	Charged with energy	158	78	164	191	112	97
9.	Argumentative	119	96	185	131	101	168
10.	Focused	164	102	134	109	48	243
11.	Impatient	133	127	140	153	211	36
12.	Challenged	104	224	72	57	72	271
13.	Worried	182	137	81	109	93	198
14.	Calm	116	107	177	175	66	159
15.	Bored	82	174	144	139	115	146

CHART 4.19 BEHAVIOUR OF RESPONDENTS IN A DAY

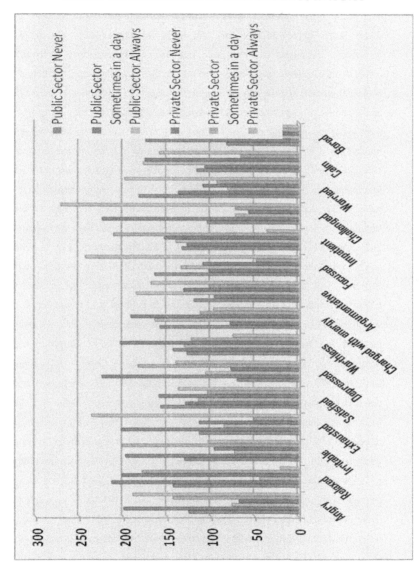

Interpretation:

In the above table, the respondents of public and private sector banks were analyzed through various behaviors. In the first statement, 199 respondents of public sector banks expressed that they get angry sometimes in a day whereas 125 respondents disagreed and expressed that they never get angry. In contrast, 189 respondents of private sector banks agreed that they always get angry whereas 143 get angry sometimes in a day. In the second statement, 213 respondents of public sector banks behave relaxed whereas 143 respondents expressed that they never feel relaxed throughout the working day. In contrary 201 private sector respondents never feel relaxed and 178 respondents feel relaxed sometimes in a day. In the third statement, 130 respondents of public sector banks never feel irritated whereas 197 respondents feel irritated sometimes in a day. In contrast, 103 respondents of private sector banks were always and 201 respondents get irritated sometimes in a day. In the fourth statement, 113 respondents from public sector banks never feel exhausted whereas 202 respondents get exhausted sometimes a day. In contrary, 113 respondents of private sector banks never get exhausted whereas 236 always get exhausted. In the fifth statement, 157 respondents of public sector banks never feel satisfied whereas 129 respondents felt satisfied sometimes a day. In contrast, 159 respondents of private sector banks never feel satisfied whereas 137 respondents expressed that they always feel satisfied. In the sixth statement, 224 respondents of public sector banks feel depressed sometimes a day whereas, 106 respondents always feel depressed. In similarity, 183 respondents of private sector banks also feel depressed sometimes a day and 140 respondents felt always that they were depressed. In the next statement, 143 respondents of public sector banks sometimes feel worthless whereas 130 respondents always felt worthless. In contrary, 203 respondents of private sector banks never felt worthless and 122 respondents felt worthless sometimes a day. In the eighth statement, 164 respondents of public sector banks felt that they were always charged with energy whereas in private sector banks 191 employees felt that they never get fully charged with energy. In the ninth statement, 119 respondents of public sector banks never get argumentative whereas 168 respondents of private sector banks always get argumentative. In the tenth statement, 164 respondents of public sector banks never get focused on work whereas 243 respondents of private sector banks were always focused on work. In the next statement, 133 respondents of public sector banks expressed that they never get impatient whereas in private sector banks 211 respondents sometimes get impatient in a day. In the twelfth statement, 224 respondents of public sector banks feel challenged sometimes a day whereas 271 respondents of private sector banks always feel challenged at work. In the thirteenth statement, 182 respondents never feel worried in public sector banks whereas in private sector banks 198 respondents expressed that they always feel worried. In the second last statement, 116 respondents of public sector banks never feel calm whereas 107 respondents feel calm sometimes a day. On the contrary, 175 respondents never feel calm in private sector banks whereas 159 respondents always feel calm. In the last statement, 82 respondents never feel bored in public sector banks whereas 174 respondents sometimes feel bored in the bank. In contrast, 146 respondents of private sector banks always feel bored and 115 respondents expressed that they sometimes feel bored.

Statement 20: Judgment of Level of Stress of Bank Employees.

In the current research study to analyze the hypothesis,

H_0: There is no significant difference between the level of stress experienced by the employees of public and private sector banks.

And it's Alternate Hypothesis

H_1: There is a significant difference between the level of stress experienced by the employees of public and private sector banks.

various variables were analyzed by statistical measures. Variables under study are:

- Psychological Factors with Stress

- Behavioral Factors with Stress

- Organizational (Bank) Factors with Stress

- Task-related Factors with Stress

These variables were separately analyzed to prove the hypothesis under this section. Frequency tables were plotted with the help of Likert's scale.

TABLE 4.21 PSYCHOLOGICAL FACTORS WITH STRESS OF RESPONDENTS

Q.No	STATEMENT	PUBLIC SECTOR					PRIVATE SECTOR				
		SA	A	N	D	SD	SA	A	N	D	SD
VARIABLE- Psychological Factors with Stress											
LIKERT SCORE ➔		5	4	3	2	1	5	4	3	2	1
1.	I feel worthless and helpless	19	103	45	176	57	64	103	29	129	75
2.	I feel Restless or nervous	58	73	39	188	42	91	125	31	110	43
3.	I feel bored in organization	63	117	41	142	37	53	166	22	132	27
4.	I want to quit the job	74	53	33	189	51	66	203	46	52	33
5.	I am frustrated	70	89	27	151	63	61	211	28	48	52

(Where SA= Strongly Agree, A=Agree, N=Neutral, D= Disagree, SD=Strongly Disagree)

Interpretation:

The above table analyses the responses of respondents on statements related to their level of stress. In the first statement, 103 respondents of public sector banks agreed and 176 respondents disagreed that they feel worthless and helpless whereas in private sector banks 103 respondents agreed and 129 respondents disagreed to it. In the second statement, 73 respondents of public sector banks agreed and 188 respondents disagreed that they feel restless or nervous whereas in private sector banks 125 respondents agreed and 110 respondents disagreed to it. In the third statement, 117 respondents of public sector banks agreed and 142 respondents disagreed that they feel bored in the organization whereas in private sector banks 166 respondents agreed and 132 respondents disagreed to it. In the fourth statement, 53 respondents of public sector banks agreed and 189 respondents disagreed that they want to quit the job whereas in private sector banks 203 respondents agreed and 52 respondents disagreed. In the last statement, 89 respondents from public sector banks agreed and 151 disagreed that they were frustrated from the job whereas in private sector banks 211 respondents agreed and 52 respondents strongly disagreed to it.

STATISTICAL ANALYSIS

Thus, the current **Null Hypothesis Ho**: There is no significant difference between the level of stress experienced by the employees of public and private sector banks and **Alternate Hypothesis H$_A$**: There is a significant difference between the level of stress experienced by the employees of public and private sector banks can be tested with statistical analysis for the current table.

Statistical analysis:

To prove the hypothesis by Statistical analytical test after applying *Likert scale* interpretation the frequency was analyzed with *Levene's test for equality of variance followed by 't' test on the above variable*

Likert Scale= Rank 5 is best Strongly Agree and that means it holds more significance as compensation parameter of employee and rank is decreasing its expectancy. Therefore in scoring, it can be observed that the rank is correlated with the score obtained on the Likert scale. The mean and maximum and minimum limits for each item in the Likert scale are collected.

The Likert Scale Frequency table used for statistical analysis is as below:-

Likert Scale Table of Table 4.21

Q.No	STATEMENT	PUBLIC SECTOR					PRIVATE SECTOR				
		SA	A	N	D	SD	SA	A	N	D	SD
VARIABLE- Psychological Factors with Stress											
LIKERT SCORE ⟶		5	4	3	2	1	5	4	3	2	1
1.	I feel worthless and helpless	95	412	135	352	57	320	412	87	258	75
2.	I feel Restless or nervous	290	292	117	376	42	455	500	93	220	43
3	I feel bored in organization	315	468	123	284	37	265	664	66	264	27
4	I want to quit the job	370	212	99	378	51	330	812	138	104	33
5	I am frustrated	350	356	81	302	63	305	844	84	96	52

Independent Samples Test										
VARIABLE AND BANK TYPE		Levene's Test for Equality of Variances		t-test for Equality of Means						
		F	**Sig.**	**t**	**df**	**Sig. (2-tailed)**	**Mean Difference**	**Std. Error Difference**	95% Confidence Interval of the Difference	
									Lower	Upper
Psychological factors with stress	Public Sector Bank	7.001	.009	-2.838	148	.005	-0.23	0.08	-0.39	-0.07
	Private Sector Bank	4.904	.028	-1.769	155	.079	-0.15	0.09	-0.33	0.02

Result: As the P value is 0.005, considered extremely significant, therefore **Null Hypothesis H$_o$:** There is no significant difference between the level of stress experienced by the employees of public and private sector banks is **rejected** and **Alternate Hypothesis H$_a$:** There is a significant difference between the level of stress experienced by the employees of public and private sector banks is *accepted and proved with respect to psychological factors with stress.*

TABLE 4.22 BEHAVIOURAL FACTORS WITH STRESS OF RESPONDENTS

Q.No	STATEMENT	PUBLIC SECTOR					PRIVATE SECTOR				
		SA	A	N	D	SD	SA	A	N	D	SD
VARIABLE- Behavioral Factors with Stress											
LIKERT SCORE ➔		5	4	3	2	1	5	4	3	2	1
1.	I have increased the consumption of tea	32	217	17	98	36	78	263	4	43	12
2.	I consume alcohol to reduce stress	63	198	27	83	29	18	226	36	103	17
3	My eating habits change frequently	21	104	29	167	79	95	106	16	162	21
4	I take leave frequently	30	186	52	104	28	29	67	33	203	68

Interpretation:

The above table evaluates the responses of respondents on the basis of behavioral factors affecting them with stress. In the first statement, 217 respondents from public sector banks agreed and 98 disagreed that they have increased the consumption of tea due to stress whereas in private sector banks 263 respondents agreed and only 43 respondents disagreed to it. In the second statement, 198 respondents from public sector banks agreed and 83 disagreed that they consume alcohol to reduce stress whereas in private sector banks 226 respondents agreed and 103 respondents disagreed to it. In the third statement, 104 respondents from public sector banks agreed and 167 respondents disagreed that their eating habits have changed whereas in private sector banks 106 respondents agreed and 162 respondents disagreed to it. In the last statement, 186 respondents from public sector banks agreed that they take leaves frequently and 104 respondents disagreed whereas in private sector banks only 67 respondents agreed and 203 respondents disagreed to it. From these statements, it can be noted that work pressure and fewer leaves are more in private sector banks as compared to public sector banks.

STATISTICAL ANALYSIS

Thus, the current **Null Hypothesis Ho**: There is no significant difference between the level of stress experienced by the employees of public and private sector banks and **Alternate Hypothesis H_A**: There is a significant difference between the level of stress experienced by the employees of public and private sector banks, can be tested with statistical analysis for the current table.

Statistical analysis:

To prove the hypothesis by Statistical analytical test after applying *Likert scale* interpretation the frequency was analyzed with **Levene's test for equality of variance followed by 't' test on the above variable.**

Likert Scale= Rank 5 is best Strongly Agree and that means it holds more significance as compensation parameter of employee and rank is decreasing its expectancy. Therefore, in scoring it can be observed that the rank is correlated with the score obtained on the Likert scale. The mean and maximum and minimum limits for each item in the Likert scale are collected.

The Likert Scale Frequency table used for statistical analysis is as below:-

Likert Scale Table of Table 4.22

Q.No	STATEMENT	PUBLIC SECTOR					PRIVATE SECTOR				
		SA	A	N	D	SD	SA	A	N	D	SD
VARIABLE- Behavioral Factors with Stress											
LIKERT SCORE ⟶		5	4	3	2	1	5	4	3	2	1
1.	I have increased the consumption of tea	160	868	51	196	36	390	1052	12	86	12
2.	I consume alcohol to reduce stress	315	792	81	166	29	90	904	108	206	17
3	My eating habits change frequently	105	416	87	334	79	475	424	48	324	21
4	I take leave frequently	150	744	156	208	28	145	268	99	406	68

Independent Samples Test										
		Levene's Test for Equality of Variances		t-test for Equality of Means						
VARIABLE AND BANK TYPE		F	Sig.	t	Df	Sig. (2-tailed)	Mean Difference	Std. Error Difference	95% Confidence Interval of the Difference	
									Lower	Upper
Behavioral Factors with Stress	Public Sector Bank	9.154	.003	8.209	148	.000	0.67	0.08	0.50	0.83
	Private Sector Bank	4.160	.043	4.071	155	.025	0.34	0.08	0.18	0.51

Result: As the *P value is 0.000*, considered extremely significant, therefore, **Null Hypothesis Ho:** There is no significant difference between the level of stress experienced by the employees of public and private sector banks is **rejected** and **Alternate Hypothesis H$_a$:** There is a significant difference between the level of stress experienced by the employees of public and private sector banks is *accepted and proved with respect to Behavioral Factors with Stress.*

TABLE 4.23 ORGANISATIONAL (BANK) FACTORS WITH STRESS OF RESPONDENTS

Q.No	STATEMENT	PUBLIC SECTOR					PRIVATE SECTOR				
		SA	A	N	D	SD	SA	A	N	D	SD
VARIABLE- Organizational (Bank) Factors with Stress											
LIKERT SCORE ➞		5	4	3	2	1	5	4	3	2	1
1.	There is a lot of time pressure and deadlines	23	98	35	183	61	94	167	23	91	25
2.	Internal communication is poor	68	135	32	123	42	67	173	14	122	24
3	Lack of Higher Management Support	35	192	37	107	29	27	127	78	137	31
4	Working condition is poor	48	165	32	137	18	78	155	27	121	19
5	I am facing Office Politics	49	163	14	107	67	82	203	40	32	43
6	Insecurity and threat of unemployment	66	133	22	123	56	103	178	12	78	29
7	There is no opportunity for growth	43	164	14	157	22	57	206	19	93	25

Interpretation:

From the above table, the responses of respondents can be analyzed on the Organizational (Bank) factors affecting the respondents with stress. In the first statement, 98 respondents from public sector banks agreed and 183 respondents disagreed that there is a lot of time pressure and deadlines whereas in private sector banks 167 respondents agreed and 91 respondents disagreed to it. In the second statement, 135 respondents from public sector banks agreed and 123 respondents disagreed that their internal communication is poor whereas in private sector banks 173 respondents agreed and 122 respondents disagreed to it. In the third statement, 192 respondents from public sector banks agreed and 107 disagreed that there is a lack of higher management support whereas in private sector banks 127 respondents agreed and 137 respondents disagreed. In the fourth statement, 165 respondents from public sector banks agreed and 137 respondents disagreed that working condition is poor whereas in private sector banks 155 respondents agreed and 121 respondents disagreed. In the fifth statement, 163 respondents from public sector banks agreed and 107 respondents disagreed that they are facing office politics whereas in private sector banks 203 respondents agreed and only 43 respondents strongly disagreed to it. In the sixth statement, 133 respondents from public sector banks agreed and 123 respondents disagreed that they feel insecurity and threat of unemployment whereas in private sector banks 178 respondents agreed and 78 respondents disagreed to it. In the last statement, 164 respondents from public sector banks agreed and 157 respondents disagreed that there is no opportunity for growth whereas in private sector banks 206 respondents agreed and 93 respondents disagreed to it. From these few statements, it can be concluded that although there is work pressure in both the sectors but private sector employees are more forced to work as compared to public sector banks. Also, private sector banks employees are more scared of unemployment and they feel that there is no opportunity for growth in their sector.

STATISTICAL ANALYSIS

Thus, the current **Null Hypothesis Ho**: There is no significant difference between the level of stress experienced by the employees of public and private sector banks and **Alternate Hypothesis H_A**: There is a significant difference between the level of stress experienced by the employees of public and private sector banks, can be tested with statistical analysis for the current table.

Statistical analysis:

To prove the hypothesis by Statistical analytical test after applying *Likert scale* interpretation the frequency was analyzed with **Levene's test for equality of variance followed by 't' test on the above variable.**

Likert Scale= Rank 5 is best Strongly Agree and that means it holds more significance as compensation parameter of employee and rank is decreasing its expectancy. Therefore in scoring, it can be observed that the rank is correlated with the score obtained on the Likert scale. The mean and maximum and minimum limits for each item in the Likert scale are collected.

The Likert Scale Frequency table used for statistical analysis is as below:-

Likert Scale Table of Table 4.23

Q.No	STATEMENT	PUBLIC SECTOR					PRIVATE SECTOR				
		SA	A	N	D	SD	SA	A	N	D	SD
VARIABLE- Organizational (Bank) Factors with Stress											
LIKERT SCORE ⟶		5	4	3	2	1	5	4	3	2	1
1.	There is a lot of time pressure and deadlines	115	392	105	366	61	470	668	69	182	25
2.	Internal communication is poor	340	540	96	246	42	335	692	42	244	24
3	Lack of Higher Management Support	175	768	111	214	29	135	508	234	274	31
4	Working condition is poor	240	660	96	274	18	390	620	81	242	19
5	I am facing Office Politics	245	652	42	214	67	410	812	120	64	43
6	Insecurity and threat of unemployment	330	532	66	246	56	515	712	36	156	29
7	There is no opportunity for growth	215	656	42	314	22	285	824	57	186	25

Independent Samples Test										
		Levene's Test for Equality of Variances		t-test for Equality of Means						
VARIABLE AND BANK TYPE		F	Sig.	t	Df	Sig. (2-tailed)	Mean Difference	Std. Error Difference	95% Confidence Interval of the Difference	
									Lower	Upper
Organizational (Bank) Factors with Stress	Public Sector Bank	.648	.422	7.426	148	.009	0.59	0.08	0.43	0.75
	Private Sector Bank	1.453	.230	4.062	155	.000	0.34	0.08	0.18	0.51

Result: As the P value is 0.009, considered significant, therefore **Null Hypothesis Ho:** There is no significant difference between the level of stress experienced by the employees of public and private sector banks is **rejected** and **Alternate Hypothesis H$_a$:** There is a significant difference between the level of stress experienced by the employees of public and private sector banks is *accepted and proved with respect to Organizational (Bank) Factors with Stress.*

TABLE 4.24 TASK RELATED FACTORS WITH STRESS OF RESPONDENTS

Q.No	STATEMENT	PUBLIC SECTOR					PRIVATE SECTOR				
		SA	A	N	D	SD	SA	A	N	D	SD
VARIABLE- Task-related Factors with Stress											
LIKERT SCORE ➤		5	4	3	2	1	5	4	3	2	1
1.	I am burdened with work	17	109	26	183	65	56	197	47	83	17
2.	Goals and objectives are unrealistic	69	115	21	167	28	26	197	24	112	41
3	My task is not clear to me	79	135	23	96	67	76	182	16	97	29
4	I am not encouraged by senior for doing well.	48	182	27	67	76	86	117	19	156	22
5	My knowledge and skills are not used properly	48	138	38	78	98	37	117	36	138	72
6	Proper time is not given to finish work.	43	91	16	227	23	46	201	31	86	36
7	I don't have ability to perform the task	21	92	43	199	45	58	96	13	205	28

Interpretation:

In the above table, the responses of respondents were analyzed on the task-related factors affecting the respondents with stress. In the first statement, 109 respondents from public sector banks agreed and 183 respondents disagreed that they are burdened with work whereas in private sector banks 197 respondents agreed and 83 respondents disagreed to it. In the second statement, 115 respondents from public sector banks agreed and 167 respondents disagreed that their goals and objectives are unrealistic whereas in private sector banks 197 respondents agreed and 112 respondents disagreed. In the third statement, 135 respondents from public sector banks agreed and 96 respondents disagreed that their task is not clear to them whereas in private sector banks 182 respondents agreed and 97 respondents disagreed. In the fourth statement, 182 respondents from public sector banks agreed and 67 respondents disagreed that they are not encouraged by senior for doing well whereas in private sector banks 117 respondents agreed and 156 respondents disagreed to it. In the fifth statement, 138 respondents from public sector banks agreed and 98 respondents strongly disagreed that their knowledge and skills are not used properly whereas in private sector banks 117 respondents agreed and 138 respondents disagreed to it. In the sixth statement, 91 respondents from public sector banks agreed and 227 respondents disagreed that they are not given proper time to finish their work whereas in private sector banks 201 respondents agreed and 86 respondents disagreed. In the last statement, 92 respondents from public sector banks agreed and 199 respondents disagreed that they don't have the ability to perform the task whereas in private sector banks 96 respondents agreed and 205 respondents disagreed. From these few statements, it can be concluded that although there is work pressure in both the sectors but private sector banks employees are forced more to work as compared to public sector banks and they are not given proper time to complete their tasks and are pressurized from above.

STATISTICAL ANALYSIS

Thus, the current **Null Hypothesis Ho:** There is no significant difference between the level of stress experienced by the employees of public and private sector banks and **Alternate Hypothesis H_A:** There is a significant difference between the level of stress experienced by the employees of public and private sector banks, can be tested with statistical analysis for the current table.

Statistical analysis:

To prove the hypothesis by Statistical analytical test after applying *Likert scale* interpretation the frequency was analyzed with the help of Levene's 't' test.

Likert Scale= Rank 5 is best Strongly Agree and that means it holds more significance as compensation parameter of employee and rank is decreasing its expectancy. Therefore in scoring, it can be observed that the rank is correlated with the score obtained on the Likert scale. The mean and maximum and minimum limits for each item in the Likert scale are collected.

The Likert Scale Frequency table used for statistical analysis is as below:-

Likert Scale Table of Table 4.24

Q.No	STATEMENT	PUBLIC SECTOR					PRIVATE SECTOR				
		SA	A	N	D	SD	SA	A	N	D	SD
VARIABLE- Task-related Factors with Stress											
LIKERT SCORE ⟶		5	4	3	2	1	5	4	3	2	1
1.	I am burdened with work	85	436	78	366	65	280	788	141	166	17
2.	Goals and objectives are unrealistic	345	460	63	334	28	130	788	72	224	41
3	My task is not clear to me	395	540	69	192	67	380	728	48	194	29
4	I am not encouraged by senior for doing well	240	728	81	134	76	430	468	57	312	22
5	My knowledge and skills are not used properly	240	552	114	156	98	185	468	108	276	72
6	Proper time is not given to finish work	215	364	48	454	23	230	804	93	172	36
7	I don't have ability to perform the task	105	368	129	398	45	290	384	39	410	28

Independent Samples Test										
VARIABLE AND BANK TYPE		Levene's Test for Equality of Variances		t-test for Equality of Means						
		F	Sig.	T	Df	Sig. (2-tailed)	Mean Difference	Std. Error Difference	95% Confidence Interval of the Difference	
									Lower	Upper
Task related Factors with Stress	Public Sector Bank	1.132	.289	2.138	148	.034	0.19	0.09	0.01	0.37
	Private Sector Bank	.008	.930	.570	155	.569	0.06	0.10	-0.14	0.25

Result: As the P value is 0.034, considered significant, therefore, **Null Hypothesis H₀:** There is no significant difference between the level of stress experienced by the employees of public and private sector banks is **rejected** and **Alternate Hypothesis Hₐ:** There is a significant difference between the level of stress experienced by the employees of public and private sector banks is *accepted and proved with respect to Task-related Factors with Stress.*

4.5 CONSEQUENCES OF JOB STRESS

Consequences of job stress were analyzed for male and female employees of public and private sector banks with the help of statement 21.

Statement 21: How does stress most often affect you at work? Please mark one response per line.

TABLE 4.25 CONSEQUENCES OF JOB STRESS AMONG MALE AND FEMALE RESPONDENTS

AREA AFFECTED WITH STRESS	RESPONDENTS OPINION					
	PUBLIC SECTOR			PRIVATE SECTOR		
	Increase	Decrease	No Change	Increase	Decrease	No Change
Productivity	129	77	194	187	81	132
Job Satisfaction	51	223	126	136	108	156
Absenteeism	46	135	219	241	53	106
Decision Making Abilities	157	28	215	183	41	176
Accuracy	106	81	213	214	66	120
Creativity	43	99	258	61	105	234
Attention to Person	112	103	185	145	129	126
Appearance	101	36	263	136	52	212
Organizational Skills	144	80	176	119	177	104
Courtesy	142	113	145	59	162	179
Cooperation	114	85	201	152	114	134
Initiative	85	136	179	108	75	217
Reliability	87	86	227	166	73	161
Alertness	129	45	226	234	39	127
Perseverance	111	93	196	119	102	179
Tiredness	146	55	199	203	36	161

Interpretation:

The above table analyses the affected area of respondents with stress. In the first statement, 129 respondents from public sector banks agreed that productivity increases their stress whereas 194 respondents believe that productivity makes no changes to their behavior. In contrast, 187 private sector banks respondents agreed that productivity increases their level of stress. In the second statement, 223 respondents from public sector banks agreed that job satisfaction decreases their level of stress whereas 126 respondents believe that it makes no changes. In contrary, 136 respondents from private sector banks believe that job satisfaction increases their level of stress and 156 respondents believe that it makes no changes to their stress level. In another statement, 219 respondents from public sector banks believe that absenteeism doesn't affect their level of stress whereas, in private sector banks, 241 respondents agreed that absenteeism increases their level of stress. In the next statement, 215 respondents of public sector banks believe that decision-making ability does not affect their level of stress whereas in private sector banks 183 respondents agreed that it increases their level of stress. In the next statement, 213 respondents from public sector banks believe that accuracy in work does not affect their level of stress whereas, in private sector banks, 214 respondents agreed that it increases their level of stress. Further, 258 respondents from public sector banks believe that creativity does not affect their level of stress and in similarity 234 respondents in private sector banks also feel the same. In another statement, 185 respondents from public sector banks believe that attention to a person does not affect their level of stress whereas 145 respondents from private sector banks believe that this increases their level of stress. In the next statement, 263 respondents from public sector banks believe that appearance does not affect stress level and similarly, 212 respondents from private sector banks feel the same. In another statement, 176 respondents of public sector banks believe that an organizational skill does not affect them whereas 177 respondents from private sector banks agreed that it decreases their level of stress. In the next statement, 142 respondents from public sector banks agreed that courtesy increases the level of stress whereas 179 respondents from private sector banks believe that it makes no changes in the stress level. In the next statement, 201 respondents from public sector banks agreed that cooperation makes no changes in their level of stress whereas in private sector banks 152 respondents believe that it increases the level of stress. In the next statement, 136 respondents from public sector banks agreed that initiative decreases the level of stress whereas in private sector banks 217 respondents believe that it makes no changes to their stress level. In another statement, 227 respondents from public sector banks believe that reliability does not affect their level of stress whereas in private sector banks 166 respondents agreed that it increases their level of stress. Further, 129 respondents from public sector banks agreed that alertness increases their level of stress whereas 226 respondents believe that it does not affect their level of stress. In contrary, 234 respondents of private sector banks agreed that alertness increases their level of stress whereas 127 respondents feel that it makes no changes. In the second last statement, 111 respondents from public sector banks agreed that perseverance increases the level of stress whereas 196 respondents believe that it makes no changes. On the other hand, 102 respondents of private sector banks feel that it decreases the level of stress whereas 179 respondents feel that it makes no changes. In the last statement, 146 respondents from public sector banks agreed that tiredness increases the level of stress whereas 199 believe that it makes no changes. In similarity, 203 respondents from private sector banks believe that tiredness increases the level of stress whereas 161 respondents feel that it makes no changes.

STATISTICAL ANALYSIS

Following Hypotheses was analyzed by applying Correlation on the above variable:-

H_0: There is no difference between the level of stress experienced by male and female employees.

H_1: There is a difference between the level of stress experienced by male and female employees.

CORRELATION ANALYSIS AND HYPOTHESIS TESTING

Correlation Analysis:

Correlation Analysis is a measure of association between two continuous variables. Correlation measures both the size and direction of relationships between two variables. The squared correlation is the measure of the strength of the association (Tabachnick and Fidell, 1989). Correlation analysis is the relationship between two variables. Correlation is denoted by "r". For example, the relationship between income and expenditure, demand and supply. The two variables must be normally related. "r" value is always between minus one and plus one (-1 and +1).

For testing, the above hypothesis correlation coefficient was run using SPSS statistical tool. Coefficient covariance measures the strength and direction of a linear association between two variables. A correlation coefficient is a statistical measure of the degree to which changes to the value of one variable predict change to the value of another.

The quantity "r", called the linear correlation coefficient, measures the strength and the direction of a linear relationship between two variables. The linear correlation coefficient is sometimes referred to as the Pearson product moment correlation coefficient in honor of its developer Karl Pearson.

The mathematical formula for computing "r" is:

$$ r = \frac{n \sum xy - \left(\sum x \right)\left(\sum y \right)}{\sqrt{n\left(\sum x^2 \right) - \left(\sum x \right)^2} \sqrt{n\left(\sum y^2 \right) - \left(\sum y \right)^2}} $$

Where n is the number of pairs of data.

The value of r is such that $-1 < r < +1$. The + and – signs are used for positive linear correlations and negative linear correlations, respectively.

- **Positive correlation**: If x and y have a strong positive linear correlation, r is close to +1. An r value of exactly +1 indicates a perfect positive fit. Positive values indicate a relationship between x and y variables such that as values for x increase, values for y also increase.

- **Negative correlation**: If x and y have a strong negative linear correlation, r is close to -1. An r value of exactly -1 indicates a perfect negative fit. Negative values indicate a relationship between x and y such that as values for x increase, values for y decrease.

- **No correlation**: If there is no linear correlation or a weak linear correlation, r is close to 0. A value near zero means that there is a random, nonlinear relationship between the two variables.

A perfect correlation of ± 1 occurs only when all the data points lie exactly on a   straight line. If r = +1, the slope of this line is positive. If r = -1, the slope of this line is negative.

In positively correlated variables, the value increases or decreases in tandem. In negatively correlated variables, the value of one variable increases as the value of the other variable decreases. A change in the value of one variable will predict a change in the same direction in the second variable. A coefficient of -1 indicates a perfect negative correlation. Lesser degrees of correlation is expressed as non-zero decimals. A coefficient of zero indicates there is no discernable relationship between fluctuations of the variables.

In statistics, regression analysis is a statistical process for estimating the relationships among variables. It includes many techniques for modeling and analyzing several variables when the focus is on the relationship between a dependent variable and one or more independent variables. More specifically, regression analysis helps one understand how the typical value of the dependent variable (or 'criterion variable') changes when any one of the independent variables is varied, while the other independent variables are held fixed. Most commonly, regression analysis estimates the conditional expectation of the dependent variable given the independent variables – that is, the average value of the dependent variable when the independent variables are fixed. In all cases, the estimation target is a function of the independent variables called the regression function. In regression analysis, it is also of interest to characterize the variation of the dependent variable around the regression function which can be described by a probability distribution.

For testing the above hypothesis Pearson correlation analysis was performed using SPSS statistical tool to investigate variables under study on male and female employees of public and private sector banks under study. The table below describes a detailed correlation analysis with various variables.

Table 4.26 Correlation Analysis of Male and Female Employees of

Public and Private Sector Banks

Correlations						
GROUP			PUBLIC SECTOR BANK		PRIVATE SECTOR BANK	
			Male Employees	Female Employees	Male Employees	Female Employees
PUBLIC SECTOR BANK	Male Employees	R VALUE	1	.443	.557	.325
		P VALUE	.000	.000	.000	.000
		N	200	200	200	200
	Female Employees	R VALUE	.443	1	.544	.435
		P VALUE	.000	.000	.000	.000
		N	200	200	200	200
PRIVATE SECTOR BANK	Male Employees	R VALUE	.557	.544	1	.514
		P VALUE	.000	.000	.000	.000
		N	200	200	200	200
	Female Employees	R VALUE	.325	.435	.514	1
		P VALUE	.000	.000	.000	.000
		N	200	200	200	200

Above Correlation Matrix Analysis states positive correlation as the *P value and R value* is significant, which states that null hypothesis can be tested with ANOVA and results are stated as below:-

ANOVA of Male and Female Employees of Public and Private Sector Banks

ANOVA							
GROUP			Sum of Squares	df	Mean Square	F	Sig.
PUBLIC SECTOR BANK	Male Employees	Between Groups	1.472	5	.294	1.010	.413
		Within Groups	58.610	201	.292		
		Total	60.082	206			
	Female Employees	Between Groups	5.322	5	1.064	3.746	.003
		Within Groups	57.118	201	.284		
		Total	62.440	206			
PRIVATE SECTOR BANK	Male Employees	Between Groups	.580	5	.116	.546	.741
		Within Groups	42.710	201	.212		
		Total	43.290	206			
	Female Employees	Between Groups	1.493	5	.299	.947	.011
		Within Groups	63.364	201	.315		
		Total	64.857	206			

The above statistical analysis of male and female bank employees states that as the F value and P value is found to be significant, thus, in the tested set of hypothesis

Null Hypothesis

H_0: There is no significant difference between the level of stress experienced by male and female employees.

Is Rejected and

Alternative Hypothesis

H_A: There is a significant difference between the level of stress experienced by male and female employees.

Is accepted and proved.

4.6 STRESS MANAGEMENT PRINCIPLES FOR BANK MANAGEMENT

1. **Make promises carefully, not indiscriminately.** At work, one should take on new tasks only when he is confident that he can manage the old ones reasonably well. One should allow sufficient time for self to think before making important decisions. If one is pressured to make a decision quickly, then ask the person who pressures for a specific time period (one hour, one week, one month) to think it over and when the time period ends, follow up as promised *(Stephen, 2014)*.

2. **Do not act blindly under pressure.** When feeling pressured, one should ask oneself if the pressure is really coming from outside forces or from within self; many feelings of pressure arise from internal, unrealistic expectations people subconsciously impose on themselves. Sometimes, others are expecting the impossible of themselves, and consequently, they will expect the same of you. Remembering that this is other's problem will help to a great extent. Trying to do the impossible ultimately makes one look foolish and sometimes even dishonest.

3. **Prioritize.** One should judge and rank the importance of various contacts in both the professional and personal life, and act accordingly. Some examples are: replying the most important phone calls first, setting lunch dates with the clients or associates who do the most for the business. One should remember that every second of life is an investment of time. If one has many different social or business options to either accept or reject, then one should rank the options in order of importance.

4. **Think benevolently and avoid the adversarial mentality**. One should give people the benefit of the doubt unless their actions prove that they do not deserve it. One should remember that dishonesty and other undesirable traits ultimately reveal themselves as long as one is alert and willing to make judgments. Just as it is naive to think everybody is honest and nobody will do harm, it is also naive to assume that everyone is out to get you and cannot be trusted.

If one assumes that rational, benevolent relationships with others are impossible, then this assumption will turn into a self-fulfilling, and self-defeating, prophecy. Adversarial, chronically suspicious individuals, while believing they are protecting themselves from pain, also "protect" themselves from valuable, rewarding relationships because they alienate those who really do deserve the benefit of the doubt.

5. **Adopt a day-to-day policy of optimistic realism**. When feeling negative, an employee may be trained to see positive facts and not only the negative. When an employee is swamped with work, he has to think that business is good and that this is a nice problem to have. When things are slower, remind himself that he has earned a break, and use the opportunity to find new clients, attend a conference, and enjoy lunch with friends or associates. One should try to realize that the mind needs optimistic realism as desperately as the body needs food and nourishment. Negative thinking leads to self-destructive action, which in turn reinforces the negative thinking. Optimistic realism represents the only psychological antidote to this vicious cycle.

6. **Be a fact-oriented egoist, not a conventional egoist.** Healthy egoists want to know the facts and only the facts. They enjoy being right not because of how it makes them look to others, but because they enjoy being in touch with reality. Conventional egoists want to be right not because they enjoy knowledge and competence; they want to be right so that others will like them, respect them, or perhaps even fear them *(Chitra and V. Mahalakshmi, 2015).* Nothing creates more stress than the false, irrational belief that one must never be seen making an error. Human beings, while capable of great things when they use their minds intelligently and rationally, are also capable of error. One should accept this fact and deal with it.

7. **Take care of the body as well as the mind.** The mind and the body exist simultaneously and interactively. Just as a healthy body is of little value if one is paralyzed by anxiety and low self-worth, so too is a sound and intelligent mind of little value if the body does not work properly. One should eat sensibly and should exercise regularly. An employee must keep his home and office environment clean and organized. Practice good hygiene. Pay attention to the details, such as dressing properly in cold weather. Poor or mediocre physical health is a major contributor to stress.

In the above pages, there is a discussion on some of the ways to reduce stress. The main focus of this chapter is on the stressors, which affect the individual and the organizations as a whole, and how to manage work stress in the banking sector.

4.7 ANALYSIS OF STRESS MANAGEMENT AMONG BANK EMPLOYEES IN CURRENT RESEARCH STUDY

In the current research design to analyze the stress management among selected public and private sector banks employees, the study was undertaken under the depicted sections.

Statement 22: Kindly rate various stress coping strategies existing in your bank.

TABLE 4.27 STRESS COPING STRATEGY OF RESPONDENTS

Q.No	STATEMENT	PUBLIC SECTOR					PRIVATE SECTOR				
		HU	MU	SU	OU	NU	HU	MU	SU	OU	NU
LIKERT SCORE		**5**	**4**	**3**	**2**	**1**	**5**	**4**	**3**	**2**	**1**
1	Seek professional help	68	84	149	56	43	71	103	136	39	51
2	Manage time	112	103	58	72	55	186	112	31	42	29
3	Set goals daily and prioritize the work	113	49	28	66	144	181	78	63	21	57
4	Prepare an action plan for the work	106	28	86	91	89	152	88	31	57	72
5	Delegate responsibility instead of carrying it alone	216	43	11	78	52	102	56	173	44	25
6	Planned break from work	159	85	64	29	63	91	69	43	87	110
7	Write stress diary	46	45	82	39	188	109	49	51	92	99
8	Complain	162	61	42	22	113	114	163	28	43	52
9	Quit the Job	17	33	51	83	216	188	101	43	56	12
10	Try to look at things differently	111	98	49	81	61	166	132	41	32	29
11	Engage in Physical exercises	207	42	21	78	52	104	54	161	56	25
12	Indulge in meditation or yoga	112	92	118	33	45	163	69	63	34	71
13	Use entertainment sources like T.V., Music	88	18	104	56	134	46	45	82	39	188
14	Engage in a hobby like reading, painting, etc.	91	69	43	87	110	58	83	161	55	43
15	Talk with Friends/Family	186	112	31	42	29	113	49	28	66	144
16	Sleep more	149	55	49	56	91	103	62	33	91	111
17	Daydream	58	83	161	55	43	81	123	106	47	43
18	Smoke/ Drink alcohol	98	76	44	69	113	164	49	11	51	125
19	Coffee, Tea etc	116	142	41	64	37	208	55	48	23	66
20	Leave the Tension at work	46	45	82	39	188	109	49	51	92	99

(HU= Highly Used, MU= Mostly Used, SU= Somewhat Used, OU= Occasionally Used, NU= Not Used)

Interpretation:

The above table evaluates a few coping strategies which help the respondents to cope up with stress. In the first statement, 84 respondents from public sector banks mostly used professional help and 149 respondents sometimes used it whereas in private sector banks 103 respondents mostly used it and 71 respondents highly used this strategy. In the second statement, 112 respondents from public sector banks highly used time management whereas 186 respondents in private sector banks highly used time management. In the third statement, 144 respondents from public sector banks never used to set up goals and prioritize the work whereas 181 respondents from private sector banks highly used this strategy. In the fourth statement, 106 respondents from public sector banks highly used the strategy 'action plan for work' whereas 152 respondents from private sector banks highly used action plan strategy to complete the work. In the fifth statement, 216 respondents from public sector banks highly used to delegate responsibility instead of carrying it alone whereas only 102 respondents highly used such strategy in private sector banks. In the sixth statement, 159 respondents from public sector banks highly used planned breaks from work whereas 110 respondents from private sector banks never used such type of strategy. In the seventh statement, 188 respondents from public sector banks never used diary writing to reduce stress whereas 109 respondents from private sector banks highly used it. In the ninth statement, 216 respondents from public sector banks never used to think about quitting the job whereas 188 respondents highly used to think about it in private sector banks. In the tenth statement, 111 respondents from public sector banks highly used to look at things differently and similarly 166 respondents in private sector banks did the same. In the eleventh statement, 207 respondents from public sector banks highly used to engage in physical activities to reduce stress whereas 161 respondents sometimes used to work out in private sector banks. In the twelfth statement, 112 respondents from public sector banks highly used meditation or yoga as a stress coping strategy and similarly 163 respondents from private sector banks also did the same. In the thirteenth statement, 104 respondents from public sector bank sometimes used entertainment sources like T.V., Music for reducing stress whereas 188 respondents from private sector banks never used such sources. In the fourteenths statement, 110 respondents from public sector banks never used reading or painting as a stress coping strategies whereas 161 respondents from private sector banks sometimes did these things. In the fifteenth statement, 186 respondents from public sector banks highly used to talk with friends and family whereas 144 respondents from private sector banks never used to do it. In the sixteenth statement, 149 respondents from public sector banks highly used sleeping as a mode of relaxation whereas in private sector banks 111 respondents never used such strategies. In the seventeenth statement, 161 respondents in public sector banks sometimes used to daydream whereas 123 respondents from private sector banks mostly used to daydream. In the eighteenth statement, 113 respondents from public sector banks never used smoking and drinking as their stress relief whereas 164 respondents from private sector banks highly used smoking and drinking for reducing stress. In the nineteenth statement, 142 respondents from public sector banks mostly consumed coffee and tea whereas 208 respondents from private sector banks highly consumed coffee and tea for relaxing. In the last statement, 188 respondents from public sector banks never used to leave the tension at work whereas 109 respondents from private sector banks highly used to leave the tension at work for reducing stress. From these statements, it can be concluded that respondents from private sector banks had more tension and work pressure as compared to the public sector bank employees and they were not involving in any kind of hobbies because of high working hours.

STATISTICAL ANALYSIS

Thus the current **Null Hypothesis Ho:** There is no significant difference between the stress coping methods used by public and private sector banks and **Alternate Hypothesis H$_A$:** There is a significant difference between the stress coping methods used by public and private sector banks, can be tested with statistical analysis for the current table.

To prove the hypothesis by Statistical analytical test after applying *Likert scale* interpretation the frequency was analyzed with *Levene's test for equality of variance followed by 't' test on the above variable*

Likert Scale= Rank 5 is best Strongly Agree and this means it holds more significance as a compensation parameter of employee and rank is decreasing its expectancy. Therefore in scoring, it can be observed that the rank is correlated with the score obtained on the Likert scale. The mean and maximum and minimum limits for each item in the Likert scale are collected.

The Likert Scale Frequency table used for statistical analysis is as below:-

Likert Scale Table of Table 4.27

Q.No	STATEMENT	PUBLIC SECTOR					PRIVATE SECTOR				
		HU	*MU*	*SU*	*OU*	*NU*	*HU*	*MU*	*SU*	*OU*	*NU*
LIKERT SCORE	→	5	4	3	2	1	5	4	3	2	1
1	Seek professional help	340	336	447	112	43	355	412	408	78	51
2	Manage time	560	412	174	144	55	930	448	93	84	29
3	Set goals daily and prioritize the work	565	196	84	132	144	905	312	189	42	57
4	Prepare an action plan for the work	530	112	258	182	89	760	352	93	114	72
5	Delegate responsibility instead of carrying it alone	1080	172	33	156	52	510	224	519	88	25
6	Planned break from work	795	340	192	58	63	455	276	129	174	110
7	Write stress diary	230	180	246	78	188	545	196	153	184	99
8	Complain	810	244	126	44	113	570	652	84	86	52
9	Quit the Job	85	132	153	166	216	940	404	129	112	12
10	Try to look at things differently	555	392	147	162	61	830	528	123	64	29
11	Engage in Physical exercises	1035	168	63	156	52	520	216	483	112	25
12	Indulge in meditation or yoga	560	368	354	66	45	815	276	189	68	71
13	Use entertainment sources like T.V., Music	440	72	312	112	134	230	180	246	78	188
14	Engage in a hobby like reading, painting, etc.	455	276	129	174	110	290	332	483	110	43
15	Talk with Friends/Family	930	448	93	84	29	565	196	84	132	144
16	Sleep more	745	220	147	112	91	515	248	99	182	111
17	Daydream	290	332	483	110	43	405	492	318	94	43
18	Smoke/ Drink alcohol	490	304	132	138	113	820	196	33	102	125
19	Coffee, Tea etc	580	568	123	128	37	1040	220	144	46	66
20	Leave the Tension at work	230	180	246	78	188	545	196	153	184	99

Independent Samples Test										
VARIABLE AND BANK TYPE		Levene's Test for Equality of Variances		t-test for Equality of Means						
		F	Sig.	t	Df	Sig. (2-tailed)	Mean Difference	Std. Error Difference	95% Confidence Interval of the Difference	
									Lower	Upper
STRESS COPING	**Public Sector Bank**	3.001	.009	-2.838	148	.004	-0.23	0.08	-0.39	-0.07
	Private Sector Bank	1.904	.028	-1.769	155	.069	-0.15	0.09	-0.33	0.02

Result: As the P value is 0.004, considered extremely significant, therefore, the **Null Hypothesis Ho:** There is no significant difference between the stress coping methods used by public and private sector banks is **rejected** and **Alternate Hypothesis H_a:** There is a significant difference between the stress coping methods used by public and private sector banks is **accepted and proved.**

Statement 23: Kindly rate the kind of Practices of Management of Job Stress available in your bank.

(a) Is there any stress management program conducted in your banks?

TABLE 4.28 STRESS MANAGEMENT PROGRAMS CONDUCTED IN
SELECTED BANKS

Respondents Opinion	Public Sector		Private Sector	
	Frequency	Percentage (%)	Frequency	Percentage (%)
Yes	221	55.25%	263	65.75%
No	179	44.75%	137	34.25%

CHART 4.20 STRESS MANAGEMENT PROGRAMS CONDUCTED IN
SELECTED BANKS

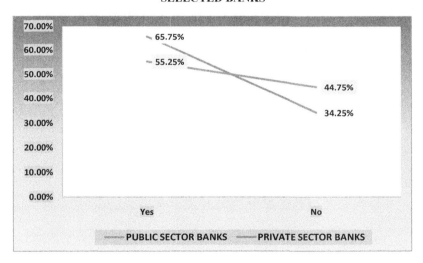

Interpretation:

The above table analyses whether the public and private sector banks organize any kind of stress management programs for their respondents or not. Maximum respondents i.e. 55.25% and 65.75% of both public and private banks, respectively agreed that they were provided with stress management programs by their banks whereas the remaining 44.75% and 34.25% respondents of both the banks disagreed to it. It can be noted that private sector banks were providing more stress management programs as compared to public sector banks.

(b) If yes then please specify how often it is conducted (Multiple Choices)

TABLE 4.29 FREQUENCY OF STRESS MANAGEMENT PROGRAMS CONDUCTED IN SELECTED BANKS

Respondents	Public Sector		Private Sector	
Opinion	Frequency	Percentage (%)	Frequency	Percentage (%)
Daily Basis	11	4.97%	32	12.16%
Weekly Basis	38	17.19%	59	22.43%
Monthly Basis	43	19.45%	84	31.93%
Half Yearly	78	35.29%	61	23.19%
Annually	51	23.07%	27	10.26%

CHART 4.21 FREQUENCY OF STRESS MANAGEMENT PROGRAMS CONDUCTED IN SELECTED BANKS

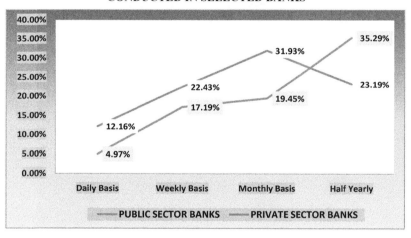

Interpretation:

In the above table, the respondent's opinion was being analyzed on how often the programs are being conducted by banks. The maximum respondents i.e. 35.29% of public sector banks believe that the programs were conducted half yearly whereas in private sector banks 31.93% respondents believe that programs were conducted on a monthly basis. The minimum respondents i.e. 4.97% of public sector banks believe that programs were conducted on a daily basis but in contrary 10.26% respondents of private sector banks believe that it was conducted annually.

(c) Which of the following means for managing stress does your bank offer?

TABLE 4.30 MEANS OF STRESS MANAGEMENT PROGRAMS
CONDUCTED IN SELECTED BANKS

Stress Reducing Programs	Public Sector		Private Sector	
	Frequency	Percentage (%)	Frequency	Percentage (%)
Employee Assistance Program	35	8.75%	26	6.5%
Breaks	33	8.25%	13	3.25%
Employee Empowerment Programs	25	6.25%	38	9.5%
Financial Counseling	23	5.75%	31	7.75%
Stress Management Seminars	45	11.25%	53	13.25%
Flextime	19	4.75%	32	8%
Ergonomically Correct Furniture	24	6%	21	5.25%
Job Redesign	17	4.25%	13	3.25%
Assistance with Child Care	55	13.75%	48	12%
Assigned Parking	11	2.75%	8	2%
Wellness Program	9	2.25%	15	3.75%
Access for Disabled	21	5.25%	18	4.5%
Training Programs	36	9%	51	12.7%
Alternative Schedules	24	6%	12	3%
Insurance	23	5.75%	21	5.25%

CHART 4.22 MEANS OF STRESS MANAGEMENT PROGRAMS
CONDUCTED IN SELECTED BANKS

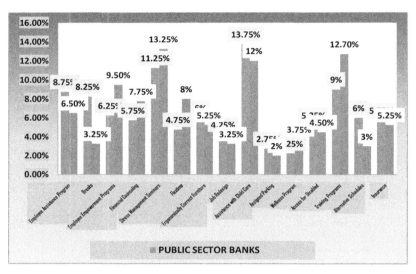

Interpretation:

From the above table, the various stress management programs offered by public and private sector banks were evaluated. Maximum respondents i.e. 13.75% of public sector banks believe that Assistance with Child Care is the most common program provided by public sector banks whereas in private sector maximum respondents i.e. 13.25% feel that stress management seminars are more frequently conducted by their banks to reduce the stress level of the employees. The minimum respondents i.e. 2.25% of public sector banks and 2% of private sector banks feel that wellness programs and assigned parking are the major programs conducted by these banks, respectively to reduce the stress of respondents. Many more programs are given in the table like insurance, job redesign, flex time, etc. which must be provided to the employees by their banks.

Findings and Suggestions

CHAPTER-V

FINDINGS AND SUGGESTIONS

5.1 BACKGROUND OF RESEARCH:

Work plays a critical role in the lives of individuals which has contributed to the phenomenon of stress for both individual employees and the organizations. Stress, at work, is one of the threats in providing a healthy platform of work to employees. The organizations have realized the nature of stress as a new age killer due to which a lot of human potential is drained out. It is associated with low motivation and morale, decrease in performance, low job satisfaction, low-quality products and services, poor internal communication and conflicts, etc.

On account of this, the organizations including banks are turning towards giving some attention to the health of their employees, not only physical but mental also, by undertaking the integration of the individual with the bank as their strategic activity.

The integration of an individual within the banks chiefly takes place through a system of roles. Roles are a key aspect of employees' job-related functions and include expectations employees have of one another and about the jobs they perform within the banks. The stress induced due to roles performed by individuals as employees at banks has been one of the most persuasive organizational stressors the outcomes of which have been found to be costly for the public and private sector banking industry in India.

The previous work in the area of stress and stress management has made available a number of variables which are sources of stress, inherent in the individual as well in any organizational setting. However, the previous studies in this area of research indicate that the stress in banking employees as a phenomenon has hardly been understood in its entirety and comprehensively in case of public and private sector banks, particularly in the Indian context. Considering it, the present study has been undertaken to add to the existing literature and to explore the unknown or less explored areas of job stress phenomenon.

The purpose of the study is to find out the key factors responsible for creating the level of stress comparing both the public as well as the private sector. In addition to this, the researcher also studies the causes of stress and proposes remedies to control stress among employees. This study would help the bank management as well as the employees to identify the factors causing stress and coping strategies to be followed. Therefore, a study of this type of identifying the stress factors and analyzing the coping up strategies among bank employees will certainly help for developing training programmes in a big way.

In this backdrop, the present research on "Job Stress Among Employees of Banking Industry (A Comparative Study of Selected Public and Private Sector Banks in Haryana)" is conducted. The proposed research work endeavors to undertake an in-depth study of job stress among the employees of the banking industry. The objectives of the study are:

1. To study and compare the level of job stress among the employees of public and private sector banks.

2. Exploration of various factors which have the potential to produce/cause stress.

3. To compare the level of job stress experienced by male and female employees in the banks under study.

4. To study the effects of stress on employee job satisfaction.

5. To analyze the effects of stress on the health of employees.

6. To identify and compare the various stress coping methods used by public and private sector banks.

5.2 FINDINGS OF RESEARCH:

After the analysis of data gathered through questionnaires, this section includes the findings based on the analysis in current research. These findings are as under:

The frequency tables of 400 employees as respondents of each public and private sector segment of banks in Haryana had been evaluated and statistical analysis on various study variable tables were shown with the mean, standard deviation, t-values, p-value, and lower & upper values at 95% CI of the differences of all the variables under study for both private and public sector banks.

The results showed that there was very less difference between the means in both private and public sector banks. This shows that the level of stress in both private and public sector banks was almost same but public sector banks are more affected with job stress due to their comparatively low pace for adapting to the new technology and trends as well as coming up with new policies. Moreover, the public sector banks are more centralized in the sense that they are not involving their employees in the decision-making process as well as the communication gap is too much. Keeping in mind these findings researcher concluded that the main hypothesis H_1 which is "there is a significant difference between the level of stress experienced by the employees of public and private sector banks" have supported.

Some of the reasons for supporting other hypothesizes are given below:

- In public sector banks, it is ordered that by the year 2012, all of the existing officer cadre employees must have a Masters in Business Administration degree , otherwise they will be offered the golden handshake, and they will have to leave the bank, which is a kind of job insecurity, although they will be compensated for it. Whereas in private sector banks, the recruitment is mostly based on professional educational background i.e. business, information technology, commerce, etc.

- These employees of public sector banks feel easy working manually, i.e. in books of accounts, but the introduction of highly complex digital technologies and different kinds of software for banking operations also contribute to the stress of these bank employees. On the other hand in the private sector, as mentioned above the recruitment is based on professional education, these selected candidates are well equipped dealing with such innovations and developments.

- In some public banks, it is also found that there is lack of required staff, because most of the staff members left the bank for much better packages in the private sector banks, due to this problem of turnover, the employees in public sector banks are overburdened, and are given unreasonable deadlines to perform a task, which also contributes to stress.

- These public sector employees also complain about the unpleasant environment at workplace, for example, too many files on their tables, pens, pencils, staple, and other stationery are missing from their tables, chairs are not placed properly, etc but this problem can be managed by individual himself.

- But for some variables, the stress level is comparatively higher in the private sector than the public sector like private sector employee complains of longer working hours than normal.

- Almost all employees of both sectors complain about physical tiredness and other health issues because of the nature of the work they are involved in.

- Although, the banks in the public sector are more characteristic of role indistinctness, self-diminution, role invasiveness, resource shortage and banks in private sector of role excess and role divergence, but the difference is found to be statistically insignificant. This shows that the majority of the role stress dimensions, which explain more than the $2/3^{rd}$ portion of the explained variance of the extracted factors; do not significantly differ amongst public and private sector banks.

Other general findings of the research are as illustrated:

- As per hypothesis, job stress had a negative relation with job performance which means that when stress occurs it affects the performance of employees negatively, that lower the stress it increases the performance so both these are inversely proportional to each other.

- Stress in the work environment reduces the intention of employees to perform better in jobs. With the increasing level of stress the employees thinking demoralize and his tendency to work well also decreases. No doubt stress is necessary for increasing the performance of employees but up to a certain level.

- Finally, organizations can change or remove the stress by redesigning jobs to reduce feeling undervalued and workplace victimization/ bullying, unclear role/errands, work-home interface; fear of joblessness, exposure to the traumatic incidents at work and economic instability. They can also change organizational policies to give individuals more control over their work activities, develop support system, shared goal and direction, problem-solving innovation tolerated, decision making distributed, teamwork, respect and personal needs heard.

- Employees of the banks should be made free from not only fear of the quality of performance but also from other types of fear-generating in their minds. Guidance and counseling, quality consciousness awareness programs, psychological support can be provided to employees.

- The concept of five day week working can be implemented in banks so that the employees can give more time to themselves and their family and discharge other social responsibilities.

- There should be proper work division in all departments.

- There should be a friendly environment from colleagues and especially the boss.

In the age of the highly dynamic and competitive world, man is exposed to all kinds of stresses that can affect him in all realms of life. This particular research was intended to study the impact of job stress on the performance of public and private sector bank employees. Results of the research do not tend towards one direction, meaning that for some variables public sector employees are more affected whereas for other variables private sector is more affected, but overall private sector is found to be more stressful. From this research following variables were identified:

i.	Personal health issues	iv.	Social support	vii.	Role conflict
ii.	Work environment	v.	Adaptability		
iii.	Job control	vi.	Organizational structure		

Personal Health Issue has the same effect for both the sectors i.e. there is negligible difference in the means of both Private and Public sector banks.

Work Environment in Public sector needs improvement.

Adaptability is to be given due attention in the Public Sector.

Reward system also needs improvement.

There is a significant difference in the means of all the variables of the study. Overall, it is concluded from the study that the stress level is high for private sector bank employee but public sector bank employee also have certain stress related with their job, and undoubtedly it is also postulated that job stress is inversely proportional to employee performance means as the stress increases employee performance decreases in both the segments of banks.

Findings related to coping strategies or stress management in public and private sector banks under study:

- The study reveals that employees use seven coping dimensions for combating role stress which explains 62.46 percent of the total variance. 'Submissive Coping' which broadly relates to putting off a situation, which one feels incapable of handling, has emerged as the most important coping strategy used by the employees of the banks accounting for 18.37 percent of the total variance. A passive approach to coping is what characterizes submissive coping dimension.

- Factor analysis has recognized 'Functional Coping' as a coping factor which accounts for 12.71 percent of the total variance. It indicates that the second most important coping dimension used by the employees is to confront the problem head-on and devote time and energy to tackle it.

- The next vital coping dimension used by the employees is 'Diversion coping' explaining 8.03 percent of the total variance. This dimension helps in diverting the attention of the individual from the problem to recreation thereby adapting to the environment.

- 'Relaxation Coping' is another source of coping among the employees which explain 6.73 percent of the total variance. Relaxation strategies like meditation, yoga and physical exercises may facilitate in increasing the tolerance for stress.

- 'Third-party Support Coping', which includes seeking professional help and delegating responsibility, is another important intervention for coping with role stress used by the employees.

- 'Cognitive Restructuring Coping' has been revealed as another coping related factor with an eigenvalue of 1.07 and explaining 5.36 percent of the total variance. It suggests that efforts to manage the appraisal of the stressfulness of the event are also a vital intervention for coping with role stress.

- Factor analysis has also acknowledged 'Transitory Reinforcement Coping' as another coping dimension used by the employees of the banks. It accounts for 5.22 percent of the total variance.

- Strategies like taking tea or coffee may give temporary relief from stress as depicted by this dimension. The results also indicated that public and private sector commercial banks do not significantly differ in all the coping dimensions. It implies that the type of bank does not differentiate the choice of coping by the employees.

5.3 FINDINGS OF TESTING OF HYPOTHESIS:

FOLLOWING ARE THE FINDINGS OF ACCEPTANCE OR REJECTION OF HYPOTHESIS (BASED ON VARIOUS STATISTICAL TESTS)

S.NO	HYPOTHESIS	OUTCOME
1.	H_0: There is no significant difference between the level of stress experienced by the employees of public and private sector banks	REJECTED
2.	H_1: There is a significant difference between the level of stress experienced by the employees of public and private sector banks	ACCEPTED
3.	H_0: There is no significant difference between the level of stress experienced by male and female employees	REJECTED
4.	H_1: There is a significant difference between the level of stress experienced by male and female employees	ACCEPTED
5.	H_0: There is no significant difference between the stress coping methods used by public and private sector banks	REJECTED
6.	H_1: There is a significant difference between the stress coping methods used by public and private sector banks.	ACCEPTED

5.4 CONCLUSIONS:

This research endeavor is divided into *five* chapters. *First chapter* is the introduction of the study. It presents the conceptual introduction of Job Stress as well as correlated parameters for the same. This chapter also elaborates stress management strategies followed in varied public and private sector banks for coping with job stress among employees. Public and Private sector banks employees also illustrated the impact of these coping strategies on their stress and job performance in banks.

Second chapter deals with the brief of the profile of banking sector and selected public and private sector banks under study in study state Haryana.

Chapter three is Research methodology of the study and enlists a detailed review of literature subdivided into various categories which finally leads to the research gap of the study. To cope with the research gap this chapter contains the objectives of the study, scope of the study, hypothesis of the study, relevance and research design of the study.

Fourth chapter elaborates the data analysis, interpretation and hypothesis testing of current research design. Chapter illustrated the empirical interpretation of all the data and also statistically examined the hypothesis under study. Finally, significant figures have been illustrated in order to identify the statistical findings of the research.

Last but not least *Fifth Chapter* consists of the final summary of findings, conclusion, suggestions, and scope for further study.

The following important conclusions were drawn from the study.

The technological growth has revolutionized the way the banking sector works and the competition is globalized nowadays because of the economic conditions. The level of stress faced by the employees in the banking sector is also growing rapidly. The present study clearly found that there is a significant relationship between the type of banks, gender, age, education, job role, interpersonal relationships and impact of occupational stress. So, the banking sector employees should adopt new coping strategies for maintaining good physical and mental condition which will improve the productivity level of the bank.

- The results of this study confirmed the assumption that there is a significant level of job stress among bank employees of both public and private sector and both the groups, managers and officers appeared almost equally not satisfied with their jobs. When the managers and officers were compared on organizational stressors, it was found that both the groups differed significantly. Managers scored significantly high on organizational stressors scale than the officers and clerical level employees indicating that the managers are more stressed due to the responsibility given to them.

- This study concludes that public and private sector employees both experience a moderate level of stress. In public sector banks, few employees experienced a moderate level of role stress and those variables are Inter-role distance (IRD), Role stagnation (RS), Personal inadequacy (PI), Self-role distance (SRD).

- In private sector banks, large number of employees experienced moderate level of stress , of which they are subject to Inter-role distance (IRD), Role erosion (RE), Role overload (RO), Role isolation (RI), Personal inadequacy (PI), Self-role distance (SRD), Role ambiguity (RA), and Resource inadequacy (RIn) and others left are those which cause low level of stress.

- It is found that there is no significant difference in role stress among the public sector bank employees and private sector bank employees. We also found that private sector bank employees experienced more stress as compared to public sector bank employees.

- The impact of demographic factors on the stress level of public and private sector bank employees revealed that employee's age, education and qualification, and work experience have no significant difference in total role stress. It is important for employees to know the sources of role stress. It's necessary that they know how to deal with stress and how to manage role stress.

- Role stress effect demographically. Employee's age, education, qualification, and employees work experience also play a prominent role in dealing with stress. If employees more experienced and highly qualified then they experience a low level of stress. It totally depends upon the situation.

- HDFC bank employees are facing stress due to lack of proper communication. Employees are not kept informed of policies and standards for normal routine activity.

- Lack of participation of employees and lack of proper working conditions at the workplace is more noticeable at SBI branches as compared to private sector banks.

- No relationship exists in the stress perception of the employees with respect to the parameters good and friendly organizational climate and fair communication.

- The most stress-inducing parameter of organizational climate is the lack of proper communication followed by good and friendly organizational climate.

- The employees of Union bank noticed a number of symptoms indicating high-level stress among them; these symptoms if not noticed in the early stage can cause serious health problems among them.

- The data analysis clearly shows that the clerical grade employees are more prone to stress as compared to officers working in the banks of the private sector. It further shows that there is a significant relationship between employee motivation and job stress. A higher level of job stress leads to lesser motivation and vice-versa.

- Pay is the basic motivational factor for employees. A reasonable rate of pay increases the motivation level of employees which is beneficial for organizations as well. Most of the employees of banks feel that they are not able to satisfy their basic needs with the pay they get from their job.

- Jobs providing scope for personal growth motivates personnel to work properly. A considerable percentage of the employees working in banks feel that there is a negligible scope for personal growth in their role.

- Unfair promotional policy is another finding of the study. Employees feel that the promotional policy adopted is unfair, which is a matter of concern.

- Underutilization of abilities of employees emerges as another important finding of the study. The study shows that a large percentage of employees of public and private sector banks complaint that they are not in a position to utilize their abilities fully to prove themselves.

- Recognition and status are important things people strive for. Most of the employees claim that their job does not provide them proper recognition.

- Rewards for the work worth rewarding are another important tool for increasing the motivational level of employees in private sector banks. But a large number of employees feel that they are not rewarded for work worth rewarding.

- Better and clear organizational policies lead to high productivity and motivated and dedicated employees in public and private sector banks. But from the study it was concluded that the employees feel that the policies regarding various aspects of the job are not up to the mark, hence leading to less motivation.

- Congenial and supportive work environment leads to a higher level of satisfaction and motivation. But the findings of the study show that the employees perceived the work environment as suffocative and non-supportive.

- Technological changes in the banking sector have taken place at very high speed from the last two decades. From the study, it was found that the employees are of the opinion that the knowledge about technological changes taking place in the banking sector is not satisfactory.

- Remuneration remains the main issue in every organization. The employees under study feel that their remuneration policy is unfair, hence it contributes to stress as well as lesser motivation levels.

- During data analysis, it was found that the employees are not satisfied with the overall policies of the organization. Policies regarding transfer, promotion and other aspects of the job are included over here.

- It is evident from the analysis of the study that the managerial level employees are more stressful as compared to clerical level employees of private sector banks.

- Most of the employees fear the fact that lack of quality in their work puts stress on them. It is found that the maximum number of employees in banks remain in stress. Majority of the employees try to find a solution to relieve them from stress.

More than 50 percent employees of private sector banks use yoga, pranayama, mediations and other ways to relieve them from stress.

- In the study, it was further found that in spite of stress, the majority of the employees' balance in their social life from public sector banks.

- As most of the employees feel that they feel stress at work, banks should take positive steps to make their employees free from stress so that they can work with optimum efficiency and effectiveness.

5.5 SUGGESTIONS:

Following suggestions are offered to the public and private sector banks under study and other banking organizations to reduce stress among its employees:

- The banks should take the initiative to identify the stress affected group in the industry at frequent intervals and to provide them an adequate level of support to combat it.

- Training by behavioural scientists should be given to bank employees to cater to the ever-demanding customers and to build a positive outlook on the job. Redesigning and restructuring of work should be done, considering the present workload and system of banking operation.

- It has been found that a higher level of education helped the employees to effectively manage the impact of occupational stress to a controlled level. Adequate training should be imparted to the employees to resist the stress-prone factors and to handle technology-related stress factors.

- Importance of teamwork and group cohesiveness should be taught to the entire staff for the attainment of organizational goals and for the building of a harmonious relationship between superiors and subordinates.

- High work pressure, inadequate compensation, and lack of security in the job are the stressors faced by the employees in new generation banks. Pay, perks and other service conditions applicable to other bank groups should be extended to them also to prevent the catastrophic effect of stress on employees and the organization.

- Proper measures ought to be taken to keep up the amiable environment at work spot like upkeep of control and better relations amid working hours.

- Establishment of Grievance settlement cell for settlement of workers hardships and guaranteeing disposal of issues rather than short-run answers for issues.

- Adoption of reasonable advancement approach i.e. there ought to be an equivalent likelihood of advancement of ladies workers alongside men representatives on the premise of their execution in the association. Rank ought not to be the main criteria for advancement.

- Advancement on legitimacy premise ought to additionally be honed on a reasonable and evenhanded premise.

- Effective motivational arrangements like prize, acknowledgment, and so forth ought to be presented and executed at customary interims to keep up greatness in representatives.

- Implementation of HRD Practices like extraordinary preparing courses of action, standard execution examinations for development of the representatives and association be led by applying cutting edge execution strategies viz; evaluating supervisors as administrators, Management by Objectives (MBO),to give uncommon bundles to workers regarding money related help, credits for extension and so forth.

- To guarantee the execution of laws identifying with working states of the worker for the general development of a wide range of associations, i.e. compensation and pay, organization, work laws, and Banking Regulation Legislations are completely held fast to.

- To sort out anxiety administration programs with particular HR improvement objectives in an interview with senior administration viz; yoga, reflection, specialty of living and different procedures of soothing anxiety be polished.

- It is necessary for ICICI bank management to know the factors causing stress among the employees as well as how they can cope up with stress to make the employees more participative and productive.

- Training is a key variable in the human resource development strategy of the banks. Training system not only addresses the needs in the areas of knowledge and skills but also looks at the need for change in the stress level of employees.

- Effective management of job stress can only be achieved under two conditions. First, the individual worker must be able to recognize stressors and understand their consequences and second, organizations must develop stress prevention as well as stress reduction techniques.

- Private sector banks are human resource driven organizations, every step should be taken to understand how these professionals are to be made satisfied and free from stress arising out of occupational stressors.

- The management of SBI needs to emphasize on the key areas such as fostering a strong work culture and a healthy work environment. It can be possible by implementing several employee satisfaction strategies and employee-centric HR policies.

- Employees being the vital resources for the organization should be properly motivated and kept abreast with the latest technology and sophisticated practices related to work. They must be developed from intellectual, emotional and psychological perspectives. Their upgraded knowledge, enhanced skills and positive attitude towards their job and organization will ultimately lead to their satisfaction.

- Employees satisfied with the organization's policies, practices and culture will turn to be the best contributors for organizational prosperity.

- The management should arrange some effective stress managing programmes for their employee working in public sector banks periodically.

- If we enhance the psychological wellbeing and health of the employees, in the coming future the organization would make more revenue as well as employee retention.

- Successful stress management training programs require the involvement and support of top officials and the cooperation from employees. It depends upon a clear plan, ongoing evaluations of progress and clear goals for measuring success.

- Professional help and effective stress management programmes if implemented carefully can help in minimizing workplace stress and overcoming all the obstacles in the growth of the banking industry.

- Ensure the justified use of grievance handling procedures to win trust and confidence of employees and reduce their anxiety and tension for job-related problems.

- Union Bank requires the exercising of sound training and development programmes for their employees.

- Findings of the present study have lots of significance for both public and private sector banks. These organizations are human resource driven organizations. They are dependent on the talent and capabilities of human resources. In order to unfold their potentialities, the organization must try to analyze organizational climate at a deeper level. They must try to remove blockades, if at all, present in their organization and create a healthy and conducive climate.

- Private sector banks must organize orientation programmes for its newly inducted staff and for them who get a promotion. This will help the employees to understand their responsibilities expected from the new positions. Failing to understand their duties may lead to a problem later on.

- Public sector banks must try to improve the quality of work life of the executives. They must be given some flexible time and some leisure hours to make them relax during working hours.

- Clerical level employees must also be involved in decision making and problem-solving processes. This will enhance their belongingness in the organizations.

- Communication must be two-way in the bank. A two-way communication process will help the executives to understand the directives given by the seniors.

- Banking organizations must organize interactive sessions with customers. These sessions will help executives in understanding the needs of the customers and yield maximum customer satisfaction.

- Private sector bank's head office must help and provide counseling to their executives to set their goals.

- All Executives are knowledge workers. They need to enhance the horizon of their knowledge. Lack of such opportunities may lead to frustration and stress.

- To alleviate the negative outcomes of occupational stress, more effort/work on the part of practitioners, policymakers, and organizational management is envisaged. It is, therefore, necessary to suggest some effective measures or programmes thereby making a few efforts that can alleviate the bank employees stress and lead to their better or improved adjustment within the organization.

- Employers should provide a stress-free work environment, recognize where stress is becoming a problem for staff and take action to reduce stress.

- Strategies like tie management, body-mind and mind-body relaxation exercise, seeking social support, etc. help the individual improve their physical and mental resources to deal with stress successfully.

- Many strategies should have been developed to help manage stress in the workplace. Some strategies are for individuals and others are geared towards organizations.

- Stress in the banking sector is mostly due to excess work pressure and work-life imbalance. The organization should support and encourage taking up roles that help them to balance work and family.

- There is a need for management in public sector banks to increase the level of social support among female employees.

- Private sector banks should give some significant power and role to HR director in order to empower the HR departments. This will help to recruit and maintain a skilled and knowledgeable workforce to meet current and future organizational as well as individual needs.

- Banks should introduce Employee Assistance Programmes (EAP) and stress control workshops according to the level of employees as the level of stress and employees are directly related.

- Management can do its job effectively only through motivating people to work for the accomplishment of organizational objectives.

- At the organizational level, there is a need to formulate preventive and remedial strategies to keep their employees away from the exposure of all types of stress. This would involve provision for planned breaks in between the normal working hours to reduce monotonous routine work.

- It can be noted that the cost of stress is not only direct but it also leads to many indirect costs. The management of stress is therefore very essential, especially in the banking industry. The most helpful method of dealing with stress is learning how to manage it. These skills when learned work best when used regularly and not just when the pressure is on. At the same time, stress can only be managed if one is able to know the factors that lead to stress.

- The management of banks should from time to time on their own train their employees on some stress management mechanisms.

- Various relaxation techniques such as mind relaxation techniques and meditation and visual imagery should be used. These techniques involve identification and controlling of negative feelings with a realistic approach of perceiving life and replacing of negative and rigid thoughts with positive, flexible and realistic thoughts for behaving rationally and productively.

- It is recommended that the management must educate the employees about the promotion policies and transfer policies and these must be followed strictly as per the norms laid down.

- It is suggested that the organization must take steps to ensure the right person for the right job. It needs a very good exercise by the H.R. department of private sector banks.

- In order to keep the employees on the track of success and retain them for the benefit of the organization, the organization must chart out a proper career planning policy which ensures the employees about their career growth and recognition.

- It is also recommended that both private and public sector banks must establish proper performance appraisal system associated with a reward system to increase the motivation level of employees.

- It is also suggested that the management of both public and private sector banks must undertake stress audit at all levels of the organization to find out stressful areas of the job to take necessary action for their elimination or overall improvement of job.

- It is further recommended that the employees must use self- assessment programmes to assess their work and to find out the areas they lack in. The organization must help them to improve such areas with the best possible resources.

- It is further recommended that public and private sector banks must establish a special employee's grievance handling cell with its branches at the district level to redress grievances of employees. However, it should be noted that the coordinators at the district level must be given proper authority to handle such grievances and refer critical problems to the head office for an immediate solution.

- In order to use knowledge, capabilities, and skills of employees properly the banks must use job reallocation. In this process, the personnel department can take the help of branch heads to know about the knowledge, capabilities and special skills of employees and accordingly take steps to re-allocate the job as it deems fit for employees and interests of the organization.

- Employees of the banks should be made free from not only fear of the quality of performance but also from other types of fear-generating in their minds.

- Guidance and counseling, quality consciousness awareness programs, psychological support can be provided to employees.

- The concept of "five days a week" working can be implemented in banks so that the employees can give more time to themselves and their family and discharge other social responsibilities.

- Banks should arrange yoga day, yoga camp, meditation camp, entertaining programs, etc. The working environment should be made clean and safer. There should be proper work division in all departments.

- There should be a friendly environment from colleagues and especially the boss. Employees should try for quality of performance rather than fearing from it. By adopting healthy habits one can avoid stress.

- Psychiatrists should be employed so that stress audit can be conducted at all levels in the organization and stress-prone areas can be identified. Thus, improving conditions of the job and alleviating job stress.

- Organizations should manage people at work differently, treating them with respect and valuing their contribution Thus, effective stress management and professional help can improve the performance of employees.

- Training, specifically related to the type of work in which an individual is involved should be provided. If an employee is well informed about his/her work, the less will be the stress and the more efficient the employee will become.

- Stress Management Programs focusing on different leave categories of employees at all hierarchical levels should be introduced so that employees can get time off from their busy schedule.

- Jobs which are hampering employee's abilities and capacities should either be eliminated or redesigned according to employee's potential.

- Job oriented training programs should be introduced which improve employee's skill and their confidence to work effectively.

- 'Pranayam' and other meditation tools should be used as a holistic managerial strategy to deal with workplace stress.

- There is an urgent need for compensation and rewards to outstanding performers to sustain a high-performance culture and to introduce incentives. Compensation revision is much awaited for all cadres of employees in the public and private sector banks.

- Public sector banks should improve welfare schemes to improve the quality of work-life and job satisfaction of their employees. These schemes include canteen facilities, education scholarship to children of employees, consumer cooperative stores, housing loans, employees mutual welfare scheme, festival advances, conveyance loans, etc.

- Open-house discussion/forums should be encouraged more and more for reducing the gap between employees and management.

- The personal competency of the employees should be used at a greater extent because IQ varies from person to person.

- Employee's feedback should be solicited while decision- making. Then only the employees could realize their significance in the organization and thus their ego can be satisfied.

It is further concluded that an increased level of stress leads to a decrease in motivation level of employees. Lesser scope for personal growth, underutilization of abilities, uncongenial working environment, ambiguous organizational policies are other findings leading to stress and lesser motivation of employees. Therefore, in order to increase the motivation level of employees and to decrease the level of stress, the organization must consider the above suggestions and recommendations. Besides this, the organization must chart out proper human resource development programmes aimed at the overall development of employees working in the organization.

5.6 SCOPE FOR FURTHER STUDIES

The time period for carrying out the research was short as a result of which many facts have been left unexplored. Due to lack of time and other resources, it was not possible to conduct the survey at a large level. The study is limited to the employees of selected public and private sector banks. During the collection of data, many employees were unwilling to fill the questionnaire due to lack of time. Respondents were having a feeling of wastage of time for them.

Area of the present study can be increased from state level to national level, as well as international level; sample size can be increased; other demographic details can be added in the future research and various other statistical tests can be used for comprehensive analysis and findings. The scope of the present study is limited, and hence there is an ample opportunity for the researcher to focus more on other variables related to stress. Future research can also be done covering a wider area and more respondents with cross-cultural extensions even across the country. Researchers might also want to look at the differences, if any, in the adoption of innovative HRM practices from developed and emerging market perspectives.

Printed by BoD˝in Norderstedt, Germany

9 781805 247654